FUNNY YOU SHOULD ASK: HOW TO MARKET A BOOK
THE HILARIOUSLY DETAILED GUIDE TO BOOK MARKETING AND PROMOTION

LORI CULWELL

Copyright © 2022 by LORI CULWELL

All rights reserved.

No part of this book may be reproduced in any form or by any electronic or mechanical means, including information storage and retrieval systems, without written permission from the author, except for the use of brief quotations in a book review.

Noncommercial — You may not use this work for commercial purposes.

No Derivative Works — You may not alter, transform, or build upon this work.

LEGAL NOTICE

The Publisher has strived to be as accurate and complete as possible in the creation of this report, notwithstanding the fact that they do not warrant or represent at any time that the contents within are accurate due to the rapidly changing nature of the Internet. While all attempts have been made to verify information provided in this publication, the Publisher assumes no responsibility for errors, omissions, or contrary interpretation of the subject matter herein. Any perceived slights of specific persons, peoples, or organizations are unintentional, except that one person. That was totally intentional.

In practical advice books, like anything else in life, there are no guarantees of income made. Readers are cautioned to rely on their own judgment about their individual circumstances to act accordingly. The electronic version of this book contains affiliate links, meaning the publisher earns a small (very, very small) commission if purchases are made.

GET FREE UPDATES!

Before we get started, I want to get you set up with a way to get future updates for this book. The world of book marketing is dynamic and constantly evolving. As such, I make frequent updates to this guide and re-publish it at least once a quarter so all of the information is the most current it can be.

Why am I telling you this?

Here's the thing– *I* want to provide you with the most updated version of this book (whenever there is a new one) and am happy to give it to you for free, but once you buy it, I have no way to send you the update. Contrary to popular belief, Amazon (or whatever other platform you bought this book on) is not going to automatically push out the most updated version of the book to people who have already bought it. That kind of sucks, and I'm trying to change that, one book at a time.

So, here's my request: please go over here and sign up for updates. Whenever I put out a new version of this book, I will immediately notify you that it's time to download your updated copy of the eBook version. To further incentivize you, I will also give you a free copy of the companion guide I created for this book!

If you bought the eBook version originally, great! You'll simply download the updated version and move on.

If you bought the paperback, also great!! You'll get a free eBook version with free updates to go along with it

So, come on over to https://loriculwell.com/htmab . There is a ton of information coming out about publishing and book marketing all the time, and I don't want you to miss out!

CONTENTS

1. Get Your Head on Straight — 1
2. Get Organized — 15
   Part 1: Your Author Platform — 25
3. Email List, Part 1: List, Landing Page, Link — 27
4. Email List, Part 2: Now What? — 35
5. Your Author Website — 45
6. Social Media — 55
7. Book Sites — 63
   Part 2: SEO for Books — 81
8. Amazon is a Search Engine for Buyers — 83
9. Know Your Genre/ Subgenre/ Tropes/ Peers — 91
10. Your Competitive Analysis — 97
11. Category Research — 111
12. Keyword Research! My Favorite! — 123
    Your Pre-Launch Countdown — 137
13. The Safety Checklists — 139
14. Reviews, Part I: The ARC Story — 147
15. Book Promotion Sites — 161
    Part 3: Your Launch — 169
16. Get Reviews — 171
17. Paid Advertising Overview — 177
18. 72 More Ways To Promote Your Book — 195
    Part 4: Post-Launch Activities — 213
19. Start a Facebook Page + Group About Your Genre/ Subgenre — 215
20. Book Marketing: Daily Tasks — 231
21. Conclusion: Your Big Moment — 235
22. What Else Can I Teach You? — 237

1
GET YOUR HEAD ON STRAIGHT

Hi! Welcome to the book that you and I both know you don't really want to be reading.

Come on! That's a great way to start a book. Total honesty from the very beginning.

Look, I know what's going on here. You've either just released a book or you're just about to, and you have a vague idea that you need to do something to get that book to start selling. However, you're exhausted from writing an entire book, so you don't really want to do anything. You want your book to organically take off on its own with no marketing push.

How do I know that? BECAUSE I WANT THAT TOO. All writers want that! I hope that happens for all of us someday! However, there is no way to control that, so eventually, you're going to have to pull your marketing game together and do some actual book promotion to get your books to start selling.

And look, I know marketing is hard and you'd rather do anything else. Heck, everything about being an author is hard, right? Writing is hard, editing is hard, and getting your book to a publisher (or publishing it yourself) is hard. You wanted the moment you hit "Publish" on your book to be the end, and when you realized it was actually the beginning, you were already done and now you have zero energy to market your book.

I have good news. I have spent years compiling what I consider to be all of the best practices for book marketing, and I'm going to tell you everything I know on the subject. Here's the thing, though: Just knowing what to do isn't enough. The other factor is your *mindset,* and you need to shift that before you start learning about any of this stuff.

Now, if you're someone who's just trying to get your books out there so you can see them in print, or so your friends and family can enjoy them, that's fine! You don't need marketing. But I suspect you bought this book because you realized you wanted a little more out of your writing career. If that's you, let's begin by asking ourselves a few fundamental questions.

How Do You Define Success?

Before you enter into this whole book-marketing game, I'd love for you to really think about this for a moment. Yes, you write because you love writing, but how many copies would you like to sell? Do you want to do press interviews and readings? Are you looking to replace your job and write as a career?

Because here's the thing— if you want to actually make money from your writing (and by that I mean if you want even one person you don't know personally to find your book and buy it), it is imperative that you shift your mindset over from thinking of yourself solely as an author to seeing yourself and your writing as a *business*. That means committing to learning and implementing business skills and practices.

If you do not make this shift, it makes zero sense for you to have any expectation of making sales. And I hate to break it to you, but that also means you no longer get to complain or be disappointed if and when you don't make any.

I'm sorry! I know! I wasn't trying to be all "tough love," especially in the very first chapter, but some things need to be said. Are you still with me? Good! Let's continue.

What's Your Why?

. . .

In one of my previous books (on how to make a website), I have an exercise where I ask people to identify the "why" of their website, and it's proven to be a pretty powerful tool. Because when people actually take the time to really examine **why** they want to do a particular thing, it unearths enough passion and energy to get them up and over any challenges they might face along the way.

I seriously believe that if you get in touch with your why—why you want to get your book out there, or even why you want to write in the first place—it will give you the proverbial fire in the belly you'll need to push through all of the technical hurdles and general discomfort of author marketing. You'll have a clear reason for doing what you're doing.

So, as we did with the question on success, I'd like you to now take a minute and really think through why you want to get your book out there. Seriously, take the time right now. Is your book a work of non-fiction that is going to help a lot of people with a problem? Is it an entertaining novel that will be a fun distraction? Do you just want to make a lot of money? Any answer is right. WHY do you want people to know about your book? You're a writer, so write down your reasons. I'll be here when you get back.

Did you do it? Are you clear on your why? Great! Keep that firmly in mind, because we're now going to sharpen it a bit by talking about some of the reasons writers often try to avoid doing this work, so as to eliminate any excuses you might be tempted to make going forward.

Myth #1: "Marketing is Not My Job."

. . .

I honestly believe that the overall lack of success of most authors' books is due to one simple reason: They think that the process is over once they turn in their final manuscript, when in reality, that's just the beginning.

Just to briefly touch on the myth that marketing is the publisher's job, it *is* true that if your book is with a big publisher, they're going to have a publicist on staff, and that person will do some work on behalf of your book. However, (and this is nothing against you, you're awesome, you wrote a book!) that publicist works for a big publisher, and most of their job is probably spent on authors like Dan Brown and David Sedaris, who have name recognition and who will sell a ton of books just by appearing on talk shows.

No, it's not fair, but this is the way publishing works.

Myth # 2: "I'm Going to Hire a Publicist, So I Don't Need to Be Involved."

If you have the resources to hire someone, fantastic! But be warned that you will still have to do the vast majority of what's in this book (like setting up your website, email list, and social media) in order to make your money back from that expenditure. The ultimate goal of a good publicity campaign (from your perspective, anyway) should be to grow your audience, not just to make one-time sales of your books. Also, in case you didn't know this, publicists will take your money even if you don't get any sales or new readers.

. . .

Myth # 3: "Marketing Is Scary and Will Push Me Out of My Comfort Zone."

Something else I hear a lot is that writers are terrified of marketing. They're introverts. They don't know how to do any of this stuff, and furthermore, they don't WANT to do it. They majored in something creative like English or comparative literature, and therefore didn't learn many of the requisite business skills to one day become a marketing expert.

If any of this sounds like you, I have good news. Despite what you might have heard, marketing is not NEARLY as difficult as writing a book. It's actually much easier, especially if you're a writer, because guess what? It's really mostly just writing, but with a specific purpose and intention, directed at people who a) are in your target audience and who actually want what you're marketing; and b) can help spread the word about your work, become your fans, and help with your career.

This can really be as simple as chatting with people on Twitter every day, writing blog posts, or sending your book out to reviewers. Or it can take the form of being an expert on radio and TV shows, and who wouldn't like that? In fact, marketing (this might shock you) IS ACTUALLY ENJOYABLE, once you get over your misconceptions about it. Plus, watching your book sales go up is fun when you know that your efforts made that happen. Likewise, when a total stranger contacts you to tell you they stayed home from work because they simply could not put down your novel, or when a group of people is reading your book for their weekly book club and wants you to come and speak to them about it, it's all going to be worth it. Trust me.

And no, not every effort you make will pay off. But you want to grow and nurture the ones that do. You can think of marketing like planting seeds every day: Some of those seeds are going to go nowhere, and some of them are going to take root and grow into flowers. You don't necessarily know what's going to happen with each seed, but you spend time every day tending the garden, right?

Besides, I think you need to give yourself some credit here. You wrote a whole book and are an expert in your field (even if that field is a specific type of fiction), so you clearly know how to absorb and repurpose information. Because you now have this handy step-by-step guide, I am crowning you "honorary marketing expert." You got this!

Myth # 4: "It's Just Too Hard."

OK, despite what I just said, none of this is easy. Getting everything set up so that your marketing machine runs smoothly CAN be a daunting task, and it can require learning some new things, which can be challenging if you consider yourself a Luddite or technophobe. But here's the REALLY good news: You're only going to have to do most of this once. I promise.

Once you've set up things like your website and email list signup, you'll have something you can apply to every book launch going forward. The pain will be behind you, and you'll be able to see your efforts pay off as your audience grows and you sell more books with every launch.

So yes, there will be some sweat equity involved, but I believe you can do it!

Myth # 5: "I'll Just Write More Books."

Look, I get it. We're creative types. We like to create. We LIVE to create. You should totally do that! Writers are supposed to write. And while it is technically true that putting out more books gives you more opportunities to make sales, you're really just spinning your wheels if you don't have a proper marketing infrastructure in place.

So, while I agree that it's great to always be working on a book, it's not a substitute for proper marketing. If you want to actually sell what you write, you're going to need to spend a little less time writing and a little more time marketing.

I think I've now made it clear that, while it's not going to be easy, the rewards you'll reap from marketing will make it all worth it. When things get tough (and they will), I encourage you to go back and look at the "why" statement I had you write down. Keep this somewhere prominent and refer to it often. It'll keep you going.

You might also want to put some things in place as a reward. Hey, you successfully set up your email list! Have a latte! Something that you can look forward to. And it's probably also a good idea to have some way you let off some steam. Punch a pillow, go for a run, scream in your car. Who am I to judge? Do whatever you need to do, because the one thing you CANNOT do is quit. You owe it to your work and to yourself. The world needs what you have to offer!

Okay, let's take a breather as I take a quick moment to tell you a little about myself, and why I think I have the authority to teach you all of this stuff. My name is Lori Culwell. In addition to being a published author, I also design and publish books, and I enjoy gardening and taking photos of weird stuff like thrift store clowns. I write for the Huffington Post, my work was once nominated for a Pushcart Prize, and in my former life as a marketing consultant, I worked on websites for some of the biggest companies and publishers in the world. In other words, I know a thing or two about marketing and publishing.

Here's my claim to fame, if you like: I hold the noteworthy distinction of being one of the few authors who can say they wrote their first novel, self-published it, and sold so many paper copies that Simon & Schuster bought it and re-released it. That novel is called "Hollywood Car Wash," and that happened back in 2007.

I am here to tell you, there was no magic (unless by "magic," you mean countless hours of work and some crying). I am not related to anyone at Simon & Schuster, and in fact, when I self-published, my agent at the time dropped me like a publishing hot potato. Yep, when I marketed that book, it was just me, sitting in front of the computer with the singular mission of finding my audience, even if I had to do it one person at a time on MySpace. At one point I even had a bunch of PAPER POSTCARDS printed up, and I walked around Hollywood, putting those postcards on people's cars.

I know. It's a sad visual. But, maybe it made you laugh and reassured you that whatever you choose to do, marketing-wise, is not going to be as bad as that. Luckily, you have many more tools at your disposal now.

Since then I've written many other books, tried many more marketing methods (none of them quite as sad as the postcards), and have helped with marketing for authors, agents, and publishing companies. Through all of this, I've developed some methods and strategies that absolutely work, and I'm here to share all of them with you. Do I think you're going to do every single thing I recommend? No, I do not. But am I going to tell you everything I know? Yes, I am. I truly believe it is better to decide not to do something than to not know you should have done it. Because knowledge is power, am I right? When you are aware of every single thing that should go into a successful book launch, you can develop your plan, based on your budget and schedule.

I have created this book as a series of little crash courses on the various elements of book marketing, from email lists to author websites to metadata development to promo stacking and everything in between. Almost everything I'm talking about will apply to you whether you've self-published or your book is out through a traditional publisher, and you'll just need to make adjustments based on the amount of access you have. By the end, you'll have a comprehensive knowledge of the book marketing big picture, plus a jumping-off point for each concept if you would like to pursue it further.

. . .

Oh, also, what's with the clocks?

One real challenge I encountered when putting this book together was addressing the issue of timing. That is to say, everyone who buys this book will be in a completely different place with their marketing. You might be just about to launch your book, you might have launched a year ago, or you might be a year from being ready. After many, many rewrites and too much apologetic language built into the introduction of every new concept (like, "Sorry if this information is getting to you too late! Try to follow along anyway or use this on your next book!"), I finally decided to just go through everything step by step as if I were talking to a brand-new author who had never launched a book before.

The clocks (and the order of the book) indicate where in the process you would ideally do a particular thing on the timeline. In a perfect world, you would be reading all of this just prior to launching your book, but if that's not the case for you, never fear. Just start where you are, do what you can, and take all of this advice and strategy under advisement for your next book! Believe me, *anything you do at any stage in the book marketing process is going to be better than nothing.*

With that in mind, I will also let you know that not everything I'm going to talk about will apply to you. Heck, I've been writing and publishing books for 15 years and not all of it even applies to *me*. Feel free to put the book down from time to time and take some deep breaths. Trust me, this is not a book you want to try to read all in one sitting.

What If I Get Overwhelmed and Want to Quit?

Listen, I'm not going to lie—this book has A LOT of information in it. Just take it step by step, and you'll totally get there!

To help you work through all of it, I have created a companion guide/workbook where I have boiled this whole book down to something like 50 pages, plus I've given you a bunch of space to take notes. I'm happy to offer you a free printable version of that over at https://loriculwell.com/htmabguide . Seriously, go and grab it!

With all that out of the way, let's jump in. Over the course of this book, we're going to reshape and transform what I lovingly refer to as your "author life." Are you ready? Let's go!

2
GET ORGANIZED

If you've read any of my other books (and I hope you have!), you'll know that I like to take a little time at the very beginning to get us organized so we can proceed confidently through what we're trying to do. I do this because I personally have a scorching case of ADHD and cannot complete a big project without falling down a rabbit hole of distraction. With that in mind, I'm going to make this chapter short but sweet, since it's going to take you some time to gather up all of this information and organize it.

Actually, who am I kidding? This chapter will probably be the most time-consuming of the entire book, because book marketing is one of those "death by a million logins" affairs. Bright side: once you work out this mess, it's all smooth sailing from here. Plus I guarantee this chapter alone will make some people quit, so that's less competition for you!

. . .

We're doing this now to set you up to win in the future. If and when you hit upon a "viral moment" in your author life, your ability to successfully convert that exposure to more subscribers (and more future book sales) will depend directly on how organized you are. What you don't want is to find out after the fact that the Today Show was trying to get ahold of you to feature your book but that you didn't get those messages because you never got around to setting up your social media properly. That would be a moment where you'll want to kick yourself, and we want to try to avoid those wherever possible.

Let's organize what you already have and make some space for new things you're going to learn about and create. We're going to be putting everything into a series of folders so you have it all readily accessible and can focus on the business of book marketing, rather than on the insanity of "What is my username on TikTok and oh by the way, what am I doing with my life?"

First, make a brand-new folder on your desktop (or wherever you save new folders). Call it "Author Marketing," so it will be easy to find at 3 AM, which is when you will finally get around to doing your book marketing. In it you will put the following:

Your Bio and Background Information

You probably already wrote one or more bios for your book (like for the book jacket), and if that's the case, dig those up right now and stick them in this folder. In case you haven't done it yet, here's what should go into a bio: your name, writing experience, any work experience that pertains to your book (like if you wrote a diet book and you're a certified nutritionist), and some interesting stuff about you that can be used for interviews. Different PR venues, websites, and book reviewers might want different lengths for this, so prepare a version that's 250 words as well as 100 words.

Photos of You

Right now, find the author photo you used on your book cover and five additional photos you can live with. Stick all of those in the "Author Marketing" folder.

You should have photos of yourself handy, because book bloggers, reviewers, and media people often want a photo to go along with something they write about you (or guest posts they have you write). You're also going to want decent photos of yourself for your social media profiles, and you'll need to put photos of yourself on your website so people can see that a real person wrote your book. For bonus reputation management points, rename all of the photos from "IMG123 (or whatever)" to "Your Firstname Lastname." Renaming your photos with your actual name makes them easier to find and helps with your Google results, so that's a free bonus. People pay big money for this kind of advice!

Here's what I mean—and I used a weird photo of myself to get your attention.

Change the actual filename of each photo from something like this:

To something like this:

When I use the re-named photo in my social media or on my website, Google will pick it up and show it when people search for me, and that will lead them back to my website to get on my list and buy my books.

I know you're probably thinking, "But I hate photos of myself!"

I can verify that after a certain age, *no one* likes photos of themselves, so let's just get this exercise out of the way and move on. Find some photos you can live with and save them in this folder so you don't waste 9,000 minutes fretting about it and miss a big opportunity when someone asks you for a photo to go with your bio.

Marketing Ideas (for Yourself)

This is where you'll put marketing ideas that pertain to things like you as an author, you as an interesting person, stuff you like to write about, blog post ideas, ideas for videos, photos you took while out and about, and so on. This is your "rainy day" file for when you have some free time and need to refresh your author platform or for when you're launching (or re-launching) a book and need some content to push out there (because it's not ok to just say "BUY MY BOOK" repeatedly). This is also a good place to put ideas for things to talk about in your weekly author newsletter, because that is about to become a thing.

The All-Important "Central Info" Spreadsheet: The Hub of Your Author Life

I declare that in the game of book marketing, victory goes to the author who is most organized and who can find all of their sh*t on demand. Master this document and you will master your book marketing life. In this mystical, all-knowing document, you will put the login links as well as the usernames/passwords for:

. . .

—your email marketing service (like MailChimp or Mailerlite)

—all the various elements of your author website (your domain, hosting, and Wordpress login)

—anything and everything publishing-related, like KDP, Amazon Author Central, Amazon Advertising, Kobo, and iBooks, as well as whatever aggregators you're using for wider distribution, like PublishDrive, Draft2Digital, or IngramSpark.

—all of your social media accounts (Facebook, Instagram, TikTok, LinkedIn, or whatever else you use)

—all of the other book marketing services and tools where you might open accounts, like BookFunnel, BookSprout, Pubby, Publisher Rocket, Helium10, BookBub, and more. Don't worry if you've never heard of many of these things. We'll get there.

Yep, it's a lot! Put this in Word, Excel, or whatever program you like best, because you're going to be opening this sucker up every single day from now on. Every time you open a new account or update one of these logins, come back to this document and update it. TRUST ME, this is the exercise you do not want to skip. You'll thank me for this later when you need to quickly update your author website with your latest book cover and don't have to spend thirty minutes just figuring out how to even log in.

. . .

Once you've finished the behemoth "Central Info" document, save it, then back it up on one or more flash drives in case you ever, say, spill seltzer into your computer, because I would love for only one of us to have cried at the Apple Store. I would recommend against saving this information online, no matter how tempting that might seem. This is the Holy Grail of your author life, and it must never be allowed to fall into anyone else's hands!

Now that you've got all of your author life stuff in order, make a new folder for each book you're going to be marketing, and name each folder "Book Title" (Wow, I'm clever). In each of those folders you'll put the following:

Blurb/Description

If your book is already out, make a copy of the blurb you wrote for the back cover and stick it in this folder along with the longer "description/sales copy" that you wrote for Amazon. Depending on how your book is selling (if it's currently out), you might need to re-work the description to include more keywords or to make it perform better, so it'll be good to have it handy.

Book Cover

You'll need a high-res version of the front cover of your book for your website, for book bloggers if you're sending out ARCs (advanced review copies, another thing we'll discuss later), for media outlets that might want to talk about your book, and for a million other things that you haven't thought of or learned about yet. Just find your cover and stick it in this folder now. Be prepared to send out your book cover at a moment's notice!

Finalized Manuscript

You'll need this to publish your book (obviously), but depending on where you are in your publishing and promotion process, you'll also need it to send out to reviewers. You need reviews to sell books, so be prepared to send your flawless manuscript in whatever form the reviewer wants it at the very moment they say they're interested in reviewing it. You can also set your review copy up on a service like BookSprout or BookFunnel, but you're going to need your manuscript (and your cover) for that too! Save this in multiple forms like pdf and ePub.

When you're done finding that and saving it, you might also want to take a moment to break out one or more excellent book excerpts, just to have those readily available if anyone asks.

Competitive Analysis

This is where we're going to make notes about all of your book's competitors, so start a new document for that. Some people like a word processing doc; some prefer a spreadsheet. Up to you!

Keyword/Category Research

This is where you'll start collecting keyword reports and Amazon Browse Categories to use for your metadata. (This is all going to make sense really soon, I promise.)

Marketing Ideas (Book-Specific)

This is where you'll put marketing ideas related to this specific book, like articles to write, and social media posts. You'll also want to include launch calendar notes, promotional email dates, a list of bookstores to pitch for in-person appearances, and so on.

Book Trailer/Other Videos

I thought book trailers had died out like the dodo bird, but a fellow author just called me out in a self-publishing Facebook Group and proved me wrong on that, so if you have a book trailer, stick it in this folder! You can add it to your website and your Author Central page when we update your author platform! You'll also want to put any other book-related videos in here so you can release them across all platforms (like TikTok, Instagram, and Facebook).

Okay, that's it for the "Get Your Author Life Organized" chapter. Go get started! See you in a year!

I kid! But please, really do this organizational heavy lifting right now, because it's going to make your entire book marketing life so much easier, and it's better to do this when you're not right in the middle of trying to launch your book. You have to take this marketing stuff step by step and make it a part of your regular life so your platform is there when you need it!

PART 1: YOUR AUTHOR PLATFORM

Now that you've gotten your head on straight and have done the heavy lifting of organizing your digital life, let's go through and make sure there aren't any gaps in your author platform.

In terms of timing, we're doing this first because your author platform and customer base (and by that I mean your email list, website, and social media) are vitally important to the long-term growth of your career, and we need to make sure all of it is ship-shape before we go trying to sell your books. Everything I'm going to talk about in this guide contributes to the main goal of building a list of the names and email addresses of people who will buy your books in the future so each successive book launch is easier and more successful than the last.

If you're using a pen name or you published your book under the name of your business, you'll need to build a distinct and separate platform for each of those entities, since they presumably have different target audiences.

3
EMAIL LIST, PART 1: LIST, LANDING PAGE, LINK

Hi! You're here for my best book marketing advice, so let's hit the ground running with this emphatic statement: **The most important asset in any working author's life is an active, engaged, and constantly growing email list.** I honestly can't think of one thing I recommend or describe in this guide that doesn't somehow lead back to getting more people on your list, so that's where we're starting the discussion of your author platform. Work on your list before your website, before your social media, and before your next book.

Was that emphatic enough? (Sorry, I get really fired up when it comes to lists.)

Your email list is what you might be currently calling your "newsletter subscribers" or "a group of random people whose emails you have but who you really need to get around to actually talking to." Or you might be calling it nothing because you don't have an email list yet, and if that is the case, we need to address that problem right now. Despite the hilariously generic title, this is actually not a book about how to market a book. This is a book about how to market a book so you can get the readers of that book to sign up for your email list and hopefully buy *all of your books for the rest of your life.*

Of course, "How to Market One Book and Use That Book to Get People Onto Your Email List So They Will Buy All Your Books for the Rest of Your Life" is a terrible title so I didn't end up using it. But that's exactly what we're doing here.

Before you roll your eyes and dismiss this concept out of hand because you think email marketing is dead or you don't want to "write a newsletter," I encourage you to stop for a minute to really think about something: Amazon knows the names of every single person that has ever bought one of your books, but they are never going to give you those names. You wrote those books and people (customers) are enjoying them, but since Amazon is technically the "seller," they are going to keep those people's names and email addresses for themselves, and they are going to email them to sell them things. Taking it one step further, we can even surmise that this is why Amazon is so willing to publish your books for free and pay you the royalties on each sale— because every book sale represents a lead, or a new customer, that they can sell more stuff to in the future.

I repeat: They paid you a royalty for your book, and they are keeping your customers' information for themselves.

. . .

Let that sink in. *Your* books. *Their* customers. See the problem? If you don't give people a way to come over from the book and get on your list, all you're doing is building Amazon's customer base with every book you sell, while you'll have to start from scratch again with every launch.

Amazon (and all of the other booksellers) are only concerned with *their* business, so they do not share their customer data with you (even though those are technically your customers since they bought your book). That is why we need to do our best to get those customers to come over and get on our list—so we can take them from being *Amazon's* customers to being *our* customers.

For me (and my clients), the minimum for book marketing is three email list-related things I want all authors to have from the very beginning, even if they have no author website and no social media yet. I will summarize those requirements by making up a dumb but possibly catchy phrase so this concept hits home:

3L. List, Link, Landing Page.

You need the 3Ls before you can properly market a book. 3Ls to rule them all!

Breaking them down, we have:

. . .

List: a place for your list to live. This is called an email marketing service. Examples include MailerLite, MailChimp, Aweber, GetResponse, Author.email, ConvertKit, and many, many more.

Link: a link inside your book for the reader to click (or type in if they are reading a printed version). This could also be a QR code if you'd prefer.

Landing Page: clicking (or typing in) the link takes the reader to a web page where the only goal is to offer them something awesome in exchange for their email. That email goes on your list.

If you don't run the 3L gauntlet now, you're going to be starting over with every single launch, and then you are in danger of turning into one of those authors who is constantly hanging out in Facebook groups going, "I published my book, but no one is buying it! How can I promote my book?" If you don't set this up now, you are going to eventually wish you had a time machine to bring you back to this moment.

Oh, and if you're about to make the argument that you don't have a list because lists are old-school and you have a bunch of followers on social media, allow me to point out a sad truth: You do not actually own or control anything in your social media life. Instagram, TikTok, Facebook, Twitter, and whatever platform comes next are all for-profit companies. They are not going to mind taking away every single one of your followers if something you do interferes with their bottom line or not showing your posts to people if they don't feel like it (or think they can get you to pay them for that privilege). When you have people on your email list, those people belong to you and you can reach them (in their actual email inboxes!) any time you want. No one has control of that communication but you. That access is invaluable to your career.

Now that I've (hopefully) convinced you that you do need an email list and that now is the time to start building one (and I *have* convinced you, haven't I?!), you're probably wondering how and where to start.

Start here: Sign up for an email marketing service, then use that service's tools to create a landing page. On that page, you'll offer people something awesome (like a companion guide or an additional chapter) in exchange for signing up for your list. You are making that offer *inside your actual book* by including that landing page link.

Like so:

https://loriculwell.com/sellmorebooks

"Wow," you're thinking. "That all sounds really time-consuming. I don't currently have an email list or anything to offer to get people on one, but I will put a pin in that and figure it out later."

I get that impulse (believe me), but we have to stop and put our attention on this right now. There is no later. You need a place for people to sign up for your list, and you need a landing page link to put inside your book. If your book is already out, you are missing an email signup opportunity with every single copy you sell, and just the thought of that is enough to make me wake up at 3 AM thinking about how your career is never really going to get started until you take this one piece of advice.

Here's the good news. If you don't have a list, a landing page, or a link yet, I have used my insomnia time to write a supplementary guide just for you that will help knock all of those out at once. In it, I focus on helping you get your head around the very concept of your list and of email marketing itself, getting you up to speed with a bunch of jargon, helping you pick the right email marketing service, and getting everything set up properly so you have that all-important link to put in your manuscript before you go any further with this book. The guide is called "Funny You Should Ask: How to Sell More Books," and you can get your free copy at https://loriculwell.com/sellmorebooks

By the way, I feel the need to point out that I just did the thing I am talking about, twice, right in front of your very eyes. You know those pictures that are a picture of an elephant in a picture that's the same elephant inside the picture and so on and then you stare at it until your brain melts? This is that. We're in the metaverse.

I feel so strongly about this part of your author life that I made the whole process free—the ebook itself is free, and I only covered email marketing services that offer free introductory accounts (MailChimp, MailerLite, and AWeber). You can even make your landing page on each service for free if you don't have your author website yet. My goal with the book you're reading right now is to send you out into the world ready to market your book, and that means having a list and a landing page with a signup form to get people onto that list. I'm saying all of this upfront before I start getting into the nitty-gritty of book marketing strategy for a reason: Don't do anything else until you have the list and the landing page. Stop reading right now!

I know, this whole chapter has been intense and somewhat shocking if you've just arrived at the "I need an email list" party, so I apologize for taking us off track like this. But you would not believe how many authors I talk to who have 10, 20, or even 50 books out in the world who have never even heard of or considered an email list. That is a tough and very upsetting conversation for some people (and for me!), and I don't want that to be you in the future! Almost all of those authors (once they stop being upset and defensive) say something to the effect of, "I wish someone had told me this before I published my first book."

. . .

In conclusion—PLEASE go get your free copy of the "How to Sell More Books" guide at https://loriculwell.com/sellmorebooks , sign up for an email service, set up the giveaway, and put that link in your book. When that is all done, come back and read the next chapter, because it goes much further into the logistics of email marketing and I don't want you to be lost.

This message is brought to you by Lori Culwell, author of "How to Market One Book and Use That Book to Get People Onto Your Email List So They Will Buy All Your Books for the Rest of Your Life."

4
EMAIL LIST, PART 2: NOW WHAT?

Great job! You mastered the 3 Ls (list, link, landing page) and now have a list and a way to get people on it. We're moving right on to the nuts and bolts of list management now, so if you don't have those things in place already, none of this is going to make any sense.

You're getting people from your books to sign up for your list. Now what? What are you supposed to say to these potential fans, anyway? We've already established that these people are going to be the ones that make you into a working author, so we need to treat them right from the very beginning. It makes no sense to put all that effort into getting people onto that list only to let them forget about us, so in this chapter, we'll put some things into place to start your relationship off on the right foot.

Believe it or not, your relationship with your reader/potential superfan starts moments after they sign up for your list. Assuming you've programmed your autoresponder to deliver the freebie you offered them inside your book (see why we needed that last chapter and the free guide to get us all on the same page? SO MUCH LINGO), your brand-new list subscriber will go right over, check their email, and receive that very first message from you, delivering the thing you promised.

Initially, they will get a series of emails from you. Then they'll be on your regular email list, where they will hear from you when you send out update emails (ideally every week). Before you start panicking, the "series of emails" part is just a bunch of pre-written emails that you program into your email marketing software once. Those emails go out to all new subscribers, and collectively they are called an "onboarding sequence."

There has never been a moment in the crossover between publishing and marketing worse than when authors have to sit down and write an "onboarding sequence," and that is probably why more of us don't do it. Doesn't it just sound so hideously ... marketing-y?

Case in point: I have four email lists, and I only just put the onboarding sequence on all of them two years ago. My first book came out in 2006. Shame on me! Think of all those missed opportunities!

Let's back up, because you might actually be wondering what an "onboarding sequence" has to do with you, your life, or your business. The sequence does many things (none of which is to annoy and bother people, because I know that's what you're thinking).

. . .

The purpose of the onboarding sequence is to:

1 Get subscribers used to hearing from you. You probably already know this, but once you get someone on your list, you're going to have to actually talk to them a couple of times per month.

2 Make sure they are opening your emails (and get rid of them if they aren't). There is a slight chance that despite all of that effort, people are just not going to see your emails, or they're not going to open them. Those people should not be taking up space on your list, so eventually, you'll just remove them and move on. The onboarding sequence helps you determine who those people are so you can get rid of them (or give them multiple opportunities to get rid of themselves).

3 Weed out looky-loos. Maybe they just wanted the freebie and they don't actually want to hear from you anymore. Great! Good riddance. Let them unsubscribe. Anyone that makes it through your onboarding sequence and is still around is a STAR. These people are a) going to be excited to hear from you, and b) more likely to buy your books when they come out. THOSE are the people you want!

4. Get you over the mental hump of writing the super awkward first emails. Write them all at once so people can get used to you, then when you go to actually write your first broadcast-type email, you won't be so nervous, because it won't be everyone's first time hearing from you.

. . .

You'll need to locate the part of your email marketing software where you can create automations. This might also be called a workflow or campaign, or some other dumb thing because every email service has its own lingo. I think they do this because they want to make it harder for you to quit them, but that's just me.

You're going to want to start by pre-programming the following five emails. If you grabbed my free email-setup book in the last chapter, you will have gotten at least one of these already from me (with more to follow over the course of the next few weeks). Feel free to model your own sequence after mine!

I've included the number of each email in this list as well as the approximate date when it should go out.

Email 1, Day 1: The Welcome Email/Freebie Delivery Email

This is the very first email the person gets from you, and it comes directly after they sign up for the free thing. The purpose of this email is (of course) to deliver that freebie and to make sure the person is getting your emails. If you notice that people are not receiving this email, or they're not opening it (and you would know this because your email service provider will show the open rate), you can try the following:

. . .

—Include some wording on the landing page that says they'll need to check their spam folder (or promotional tab, if they have Gmail).

—Verify your author website domain (if you have a website) with the email service provider so your list receives emails from you@yourfirstnamelastname.com. The authority of an actual domain can make your deliverability rate higher.

Email 2, Day 3-5: The "Hi! It's Me Again! Just Verifying That You Got the Freebie!" Email

This email is the next one in the sequence, and it goes out three-to-five days after the initial welcome email. The purpose is once again two-fold. First and foremost, you want to make sure the person actually got the thing you were offering, because we are good and honest people that do the things we say we're going to do. I also like to use this email to share a personal anecdote about myself or something that relates to the subject matter, so that the recipient knows I'm a real person.

I'm not kidding about this. My most popular anecdotal email is about a terrible review I once got. People think it's really funny.

I also ask a question at the end of this email—and surprisingly, I get a lot of replies! You can ask a funny question about something you think is going to elicit a passionate reply, like "Cats or dogs?", "City or country?", "Cold weather or hot?" You can also go deeper into your subject matter with the question. In one of my sequences, I ask people to tell me their biggest problem with book marketing, which has sparked some lively conversations.

Email 3, Day 7, The "Here's Where You Can Find Me in Other Places" Email

The third email in the sequence happens a week after the person signs up. In it, you can tell the person more about your social media (like, where else they can find you), point them back to your website, or tell them something that's going on with you.

Note that we're three emails and one week in and I have not said anything about trying to get anyone to buy anything. We're getting there, but come on! These people are brand new, and the point of this whole exercise is to get people used to you and hopefully engage them in conversation. We are not trying to be gross and salesy.

Email 4, Day 14, The "Call to Action" Email

The fourth email in the sequence comes two weeks after the person signs up, and it should send them to a link to do something (like to review your book). I've covered that in Chapter 17, "Get Reviews," complete with some sample copy!

Email 5, Day 21, The "Fill in the Blank" Email

. . .

This is the fifth and final email in the sequence, and you can decide what you want this one to focus on. You can direct readers over to join your ARC team over at BookSprout if you have one of those (and if not, we'll be covering that in Chapter 14), or put them into a whole separate new list of "street team" readers who will receive advanced copies and ideally leave reviews. You can also feel free to give them links to any other books you have for sale.

And that's it! By the time subscribers make it through all of those emails, they will either be fine with hearing from you again, or they will have politely shown themselves out by unsubscribing. Either way is great.

Current Subscribers: What About the People Who Are Already on Your List?

Obviously, you're not going to be able to put all of your existing subscribers through your fantastic new onboarding sequence (even though it would be so nice if you could). However, I know this is a lot of effort and I want you to get the most bang for your buck out of everything, so for that reason, I will advise you to take the copy from emails 2-6 and use them in a series of weekly update emails, starting the day you get the whole sequence set up. That way every single person on your list will be on the same page.

Care and Feeding of Your Email List

. . .

You'll be thrilled to know that once this setup part is over, there are only a couple of things that you need to do with your list on a regular basis. Here they are!

1. Get people on it! I've already mentioned the main way authors get people onto their email lists (through the link magnet link in your book), but be sure to also include links in all of your social media profiles, book sites, and of course on your author website. Any time you are interacting on social media, you want to give whoever you're interacting with the chance to get on that list. If you're using BookFunnel to deliver your lead magnet, definitely participate in book promos and author swaps once you get some people on your list. You'll also pick up some subscribers from paid promos in which you put your books when they're free or discounted. Keep that list growing however you can!

2. Talk to it! From now on, send out an interesting weekly (or at least monthly) email, just updating people about what's going on with you and generally being the interesting person that you are. This will be no problem for you since a) you are a writer, and b) because you made it through setting up the list itself and the landing page in the last chapter and the onboarding sequence in this one and are now quite familiar with the inner workings of your chosen email service provider and can easily knock out a one-off email. Be sure to put this on your calendar, because if you wait too long to talk to your list, it will become stale and the people on it will forget about you. They will not be there for you when you need them, because you were not there for them.

If you're stumped as to what to say to people every week, look no further than your own life and social media. Take the topics and photos and re-write those into a summary of your week. Note that I do NOT mean you should email people a list of links to blog posts and photos. Give them something to actually open and read, like a little life digest. Every email does not have to be about you and your fabulous writing career. This is why you made the "Marketing Ideas" folder back in Chapter 2.

3. Clean it! Every once in a while (hopefully at regular intervals), you will want to go through your list and sort it by people who haven't opened the last five emails. Give these people one last chance to re-engage by checking to see if they open one more weekly email. If they don't, purge them like the dead weight they are.

Don't take any of this personally. Chances are, these people are not even seeing your emails (because of deliverability issues with their email service), so they don't even know they're dissing you. Also, subscriber numbers (over a certain basic amount like 1,000) count toward subscription fees, and you don't need to be paying for someone who is not helping you grow your business. Harsh but true!

4. Back it up! A smart person in a self-publishing Facebook group I belong to recently called the email list "the only real estate an author truly owns," and I totally agree. Since it is the most important thing in our author lives, we should back up our lists with the same frequency we back up our computers, am I right?

You ARE backing up your computer regularly, right? If not, please go do that now. I'm serious.

. . .

We need to back up our lists because ultimately, the people on them are the lifeblood of our business and we need to be able to take them with us, should we ever want to switch email marketing services. Stuff happens—you could get into a misunderstanding with your email provider over billing, someone on their side could hit the wrong button and delete your account, or you could forget your password and lose the phone you used for two-factor authentication (this is currently happening to a person I know!). I want your author life to grow and to go as smoothly as possible, so I'm suggesting that once a month, you go into your email service provider and download all of the emails on your list into a spreadsheet.

If you're now super into the concept of email marketing and want to know more, I've put some additional resources over at: https://bookpromotion.com/email

If you're good with your email list setup and onboarding sequence, let's move on to your author website!

5
YOUR AUTHOR WEBSITE

Now that you have your email list/lead magnet/landing page/newsletter situation worked out (well done!) and you've put that all-important signup link inside your book, we can move on to your website. You're feeling empowered, right? Those last two chapters were a heavy lift, but you're doing this!

Now's the time to talk about your website, so let's get in there. Your author website (www.firstnamelastname.com) is the "mothership" of your author life—one centralized hub of internet property where people can go to read your latest blogs or articles, contact you for interviews, find out more about you and your books, and (perhaps most importantly) get on your list! I actually have so much to say about websites, I wrote a whole other book about them (which you can find at https://loriculwell.com/website book), but I am also condensing all of this knowledge into one chapter for your convenience.

. . .

I can't imagine that you're still on the fence about whether or not to make an author website if you don't have one already, but just in case, here are some reasons why I think all authors need a website. Unsurprisingly, something like 80% of these points include a mention of getting people to join your email list.

Reasons Why You Really Do Need an Author Website

1. You need one centralized place for your author brand. Remember, we're trying to get people to leave booksellers' worlds and come over to yours, so you need to look like you have your sh*t together.

2. You want people who love your books to tell their friends about you, and some people will do that by mentioning your name and your website. It's going to happen, if it's not happening already. Make sure there's something there when people go looking for you online.

3. If you're on social media at all, you want to maximize that time and give people the opportunity to follow your profile link to your website and get on your list.

4. You want people who Google you to find your website and get on your list.

5. You want people who want to know something about your subject matter to Google you, find you, interview you, and feature your books. This will get more people to join your list, and your website is the place where they'll start.

6. Even if you have a zillion followers on one or more social media platforms, those platforms don't belong to you. You need those people to come over to your website and get on your list so you can

contact them even if Facebook or Instagram take away your account.

7. You need a place to put your random writing that hasn't taken the form of a whole book yet (like in a blog). The purpose of this is to blow people away with your writing and get them to join your list. This is also where you can start talking about your upcoming releases, do your cover reveals, and link people over to things like GoodReads giveaways, ARC review campaigns, and so on. You can't rely on social media for that because there are a zillion platforms and everyone has a different one they prefer, so your best bet is to write one post and syndicate that out to your social media.

8. If you think you're ever going to want to sell signed copies of your books (or anything else, for that matter) you'll need a place to do that. Your website is that place.

Are you convinced? Great!

If you already have your site set up and just want to skim this chapter just to make sure you have everything in order, that totally works. If you do not already have a website set up (for yourself as an author and for any pseudonyms you're writing under), get on that now!

Your Author Website Checklist

. . .

I want your website to be the best possible reflection on you and give you the most support for your career, so here is my checklist for what I'd like to see on every author site:

1. Your own firstnamelastname.com domain. This is important because you want to be sure that you own and are in control of all of your content (as well as your Google results). If your website is on a free platform like Blogger or Wordpress.com, technically your content belongs to them and they can erase it anytime they want. Not good! If you haven't done it already, go over to NameCheap and register your firstnamelastname.com domain. I'm emphasizing this because I've found that some authors are still using old websites on free platforms or from books, blogs, or businesses that don't really match their branding anymore. Now's the time to start fresh with your own firstnamelastname.com, set that up properly, and build from there. You can redirect old book websites over to this main site.

2. An email signup form (or popup). You didn't think I was going to miss an opportunity to get people onto your list, did you? We've already been over the fact that I think the list is the most important component of your author life. So how do you get people to sign up? I recommend a few ways. First, you can straight-up offer people free stuff, like a free book, an add-on report or chapter that will help them with something you talk about in one of your books, or a free bonus of your choosing. Also, be sure to put a signup checkbox on your "Contact Us" page.

3. An "About" page with your bio, your "origin story" as a writer, and your FAQ. Grab one of your bios from your "stuff about me" folder and stick it on your website. You just want to tell people a

little about yourself to get them interested in you and your books. Make sure you express your interests in your bio and on your social media, even if these interests don't have anything to do with your book directly. If you love flowers, or knitting, or cars, or miniature goats, talk about that. Give people a way to relate to you so they will root for you and want to buy all of your books!

4. Your blog. Your site should have a blog with an RSS feed (so it stays fresh for Google and keeps your name solidly on page one of search engine results for your name) and you should try to keep it updated with your latest announcements and thoughts (though please make sure to remove the actual dates so it continues to look current). It's great if you've started a blog in a free location, but once you've established your domain and website, you'll want to start pulling the content over to your site's blog instead (or at least provide links to your posts) for the purpose of establishing your website's RSS feed. You can also use syndication services like www.dlvr.it or www.ifttt.com to syndicate your blog posts so that they go out to your social media accounts. Don't forget to pull your blog's feed through your Amazon Author Central (coming up in Chapter 7).

5. Your photo. Be sure to have a photo on your site so that potential readers can connect a face with your name. Use the photos from your book, use a selfie, use old photos, etc, because people do want to put a name with a face. Again, I realize that most people don't like photos of themselves. When you become a bestselling author, you can have professional shots done, but until then, just find something you can live with and move on. If you absolutely can't get your head around a photo of any kind, use a cartoon-type illustration or a drawing. Fiverr has many people who can make this type of thing for you.

. . .

6. Links to your social media. Make it easy for people to follow you on whatever social media they use the most. That way they will hopefully read your content, love it, and find their way back to your site so they can get on your list and buy your books! If you made your website with Wordpress (.org) you can use a plugin like Jetpack or Social Icons Widget.

7. Your books. Make it easy for people to buy your books once they get to your website. Include clickable bookseller logos beneath each book that go straight to the book itself on the bookseller website. Use https://books2read.com/ to create the code for multiple booksellers.

8. Press. This is where you'll put links to interviews, articles that you've written (or that are written about you), and media such as radio, podcasts, or TV appearances. This section will be a work in progress, so don't fret about it if you don't have many media links to start. Instead, use the space to put up a mini press kit about yourself. That should include your photo and bio, areas of expertise, and bullet points that you can discuss in an interview. Make sure your name and photo are prominently displayed (and if your name is hard to pronounce, sound it out phonetically or include audio/ video of you pronouncing it). This is where producers, editors, and other media people are going to be looking, so make sure everything is super clear! Help them help you!

9. Contact information. Make it easy for readers to get in touch with you (or your agent). Include a "Contact Us" form or your email address, your agent's contact info, and links to your social

media. If you're on WordPress, Contact Form 7 is a great plugin for this: https://wordpress.org/plugins/contact-form-7/

Also, make sure to include a place on the Contact Us form for people to opt in to your email list.

10. Analytics. If you're not doing this already, you should absolutely start measuring traffic to your site. Google Analytics (http://www.google.com/analytics) is an easy and free way to do this. You'll just need to sign up for an account and put the code into your website (or have your webmaster do it for you). Even if you don't want to do this, you should definitely call your website's hosting company and get them to point you toward your free site stats" which they are assuredly tracking somewhere on your site.

11. Look and feel. I would love for your website to match whatever brand you're going for as a person and author, and for that branding (and its colors) to extend throughout all of your social media. Short of that, I will settle for it not being a garish eyesore that drives people away. Try to keep it as simple as possible. WordPress has some great author-focused themes, so maybe start there. Here's a list: https://wpforms.com/best-wordpress-themes-for-authors/

12. Functionality. This is something that probably goes without saying, but I'm going to say it anyway. PLEASE make sure everything on your website is spelled correctly, that all the links work, and that your site works on mobile. What you don't want is to have your website convince people NOT to buy your books. When in doubt, keep it simple. Always proofread!

. . .

Was that a quick enough list? I know, we've covered a lot of ground here, but I just wanted to give you an overview of all the stuff I would like to see on your website. Start where you are, use what you have, do what you can.

Next up: your social media life!

6

SOCIAL MEDIA

OK, you've gotten everything in your "author foundation" set up properly and your email list is hopefully growing by the day (or at least is set up to start doing so). The good news is, you only have to set a lot of this stuff up once, so the next time you go through this book, you can skip this whole section. Yay!

Now we're going to talk about your social media life, and because I know you're probably already cringing and rolling your eyes, I have some really good news for you! I'm not one of those marketing experts who thinks you should "hustle your book" non-stop on social media, so that's not what this chapter is about. Contrary to what some experts will tell you, a big social media following is actually no guarantee that you're going to make book sales, which is why I don't put that much emphasis on it in my book marketing methodology.

. . .

I said what I said! This might be an unpopular opinion, but I don't think you can rely on social media alone to sell books. In fact, I'm sure of it. I know this statement is going to anger a lot of people (especially people that sell social media services to authors), so I will issue a challenge to any author who relies solely on social media alone for book sales—please prove me wrong! If you can verify that you make all of your book sales with social media alone (no email list or paid ads), I will not only give you $100, but I will eat my words and change the contentious statements in this book.

Am I saying I don't think authors should be on social media at all?

Of course not. That would be terrible advice, and I don't give terrible advice. You need social media profiles for many reasons– to take up "reputation management" slots in Google when people search for you, to funnel potential readers over to your website and email list, and to serve as syndication elements for things like book announcements and blog posts. In that way, your social media IS going to get you some sales, and should absolutely be part of your author life.

Here's a list of the major social media sites where I think you should at least have a presence, as well as a few fun facts about each and some ways you might use it to further your author career. Make sure you have all of that author marketing stuff (like photos and bio info) from Chapter 2 handy, because we're going to be making and updating some accounts. If you already have accounts on these platforms, go ahead and log in to all of them as I go through this list, because we're going to do some syndicating at the end of the chapter and I don't want you to be annoyed that I didn't warn you.

. . .

1. **Twitter:** a "microblogging platform" where you engage with people, share links and photos, and quickly get into arguments. Twitter has a target demographic of 25-34, and is generally considered t a dumpster fire. I'm not going to tell you that you HAVE to get on Twitter every single day—and if you already hate it, that's probably not going to work anyway. I do want you to have a Twitter profile, though, because at least some of your readers like Twitter and I want them to be able to find you and get ahold of you if that is how they like to communicate.

2. **Facebook** (sorry, no one is calling it Meta) is still the largest social media platform out there (2.93 billion monthly active users as of 2022) so you can't really ignore it, even if you think it's "just for GenXers and Boomers."

In addition to your Facebook profile, where you interact with your friends and family and share cat memes, you'll need a Facebook PAGE that contains public-facing information about you as an author. Your Facebook profile is really not supposed to be used for marketing purposes (although, the occasional link telling people your book is available is probably fine), so a page is what Facebook wants you to do if you are a "public figure," or are trying to market something.

If Facebook is your social media of choice and you want to build your audience over there even further, consider starting a fan page or group for your genre. (I've covered that at length in Chapter 20). Also, you'll need a Facebook account if you want to run Facebook ads for your book (or for yourself).

3. **Instagram** is for photos (and now video), and it has 2 billion monthly active users, 62% of whom are between the ages of 18 and 34. If you write YA, you're probably already all over Instagram, but even if you write nonfiction books about fish, you probably need to have a presence there. If you happen to want Instagram book reviewers (or "BookStagrammers") to consider reviewing your book, you'll need an Instagram account to be able to message them, and they are more likely to want to cover your book if you look like a real person with some actual followers. Also, if they end up loving your book and wanting to shout it out, they will do that by tagging you on Instagram.

Even if you didn't understand a single word in the last paragraph (which is fine—we haven't gotten to book reviewers yet), suffice it to say that the sooner you set your Instagram up and get it looking decent, the better.

4. **TikTok** now has 1 billion users, so you're going to have to stop ignoring it. I know, you think it's for teenagers doing dance routines, and you are not wrong. However, BookTok (the book community on TikTok) is rapidly growing, and authors are using it to sell books. If you want BookTokers to consider your book, you'll need to get on TikTok to talk to them. Plus, if you like making short videos even a little bit, there is massive potential on BookTok.

5. **YouTube** has 2.6 billion users, at least some of whom are looking for new books to read. If you are the kind of author who enjoys making videos, by all means, start a YouTube channel! YouTube is one of the most popular search engines in the world,

and it can absolutely help you sell more books. Your YouTube channel doesn't have to be all about you—in fact, it can be about your genre! Example: if you write cozy mysteries, start a channel reviewing cozy mysteries. At least you know that anyone who watches those videos likes cozy mysteries, so you'll have a built-in audience when you're ready to promote your book.

Another way to use YouTube is to approach BookTubers for reviews, and once again, they are more likely to look favorably upon a request that comes from within their chosen platform.

6. Pinterest (and the pins that people pin to Pinterest) has 433 million users and still holds a lot of weight with Google, so set up a profile and pin all of your book covers even if you're never going back there again (although, if your target audience is middle-aged women, get to know Pinterest because they are all hanging out over there). I guess what I'm saying is, if you write anything "cozy," come to peace with Pinterest. Set up some boards about your genre and pin some of your favorite books in there. Look in the "interests and hobbies" list you made in Chapter 2 (because I know you've forgotten your own name by now) and create some boards around those topics. Pin some stuff to those boards. Be sure to put a link in your profile that goes back to your author website so people can get on your list!

One nice thing about Pinterest is that you're not technically on there to engage with people, so it's perfect for introverted writers who don't really want to (ever) reply back to comments or talk to people. Just make cool pins (using something like Canva) and consistently pin a lot of stuff, and your Pinterest account will start driving people over to your books.

. . .

7. You probably have a **LinkedIn** account if you've ever looked for a job, so go ahead and update it with your author website link and book information. Did you know you can add "publications" to LinkedIn? If you are comfortable with your co-workers (or potential employers) knowing about your author life, definitely go over and update your LinkedIn profile with that information. LinkedIn will be very useful to you if you write nonfiction, especially if that nonfiction happens to be related to your line of work (like me!). LinkedIn may only have 810 million users, but those users are more likely to be grownups with credit cards, so don't overlook this source of potential leads.

If you are a nonfiction author and I now have your full attention because you had not considered LinkedIn as a way to help you sell more books, here are some other things you can do to network and grow your audience:

—Join groups. There are 2 million+ groups on LinkedIn, all of which are a great opportunity for you to show off your expertise by answering questions and engaging in discussions.

—Post photos, articles, and videos. These features don't get used a ton on LinkedIn, so anything you post has a better chance of being noticed.

— Post frequent updates. LinkedIn is a social media platform that is woefully underutilized because people hardly even know it exists, so everything you post is pretty much guaranteed to be seen. Seriously!

8. **Reddit** is especially great for people who write nonfiction, because you can be in various subreddits all day long, being helpful and answering people's questions. A certain number of those people you help are going to follow you, and some of them will even follow the link in your profile that goes back to your author website and the landing page to buy your books and sign up for your list.

Reddit is primarily used anonymously, so if that's how you've been using it, you'll need to start a new account with your "authorname" username and engage using that.

If you're on a roll with creating social media accounts and want to keep going, I'm here for that! To check the availability of your author name on what seems like every social media platform in the entire world, please visit Knowem, at http://knowem.com. If you are so inclined (or you have a teenager on summer break who owes you some work hours), feel free to register your own name on as many of these properties as you'd like. And remember: *Always* link them back to your main website.

Syndication

This next step is going to hopefully save you a bunch of time and make this whole chapter worth it. Our next stop is IFTTT, which stands for "If This Then That." Because you want to try to get the most bang for your social media buck, you'll want to go over to IFTTT and set up one or more "Applets," which will distribute your content throughout multiple social media channels. You can set up five applets with the free plan, which is more than enough to get you started. If you love the automation functionality and want to do more, $5 per month will get you 20 applets.

The applets you make are going to depend on what kinds of content you primarily publish. If you're a "mostly words" kind of person, for example, and you regularly post stuff to your blog, make one that takes your blog posts and reposts them to your Facebook fan page. If you're photo-focused and you're mostly on Instagram, make one that takes your IG photos and reposts them as native posts on Twitter. If you make videos, make your TikToks into Insta reels and YouTube shorts. This part of the setup process is about taking what you already do and making it count for two or three times the work. This will make you feel much more productive when you begrudgingly update your blog and social media.

That's it (for now!). As long as you have a website and are interacting with people on social media on a regular basis, you will be building your audience in anticipation of your book launch (or sending people back to your website to get on your list and buy your book).

7
BOOK SITES

This is it! The last step in setting up your author (or business) platform. We're about to start actually working on your books, I promise!

Now that we have your author platform and social media life mostly under control, we're turning our attention to some websites where you might not even know you already have a presence. I've grouped Amazon Author Central, GoodReads, and BookBub together as book-related sites because all of them focus on books and probably already have collections of your books on them, and because I wanted to give you a break from filling out social media profiles and talking about yourself, which is pretty much all you did in that last chapter.

In this chapter, we're going to pick some proverbial low-hanging fruit and hit up some websites that already have our books on them where we'll claim and verify our profiles, and flesh out our information so we can leverage their already-existing traffic for our benefit. For this exercise, you'll still need that amazing "Author Marketing" folder from Chapter 2. Make sure you have all of your book covers and links handy in case you end up needing to add your books to any of these sites. Our goal here is to make sure your whole author platform is represented on each one of these sites, because you likely have a presence on all of them anyway. Might as well fully optimize anything you can control!

We'll start with Amazon, of course, because Amazon is the center of all of our author lives whether we want to admit it or not.

Amazon Author Central

If you've published anything previously (even with another publisher), you already have an Amazon Author Central profile in Amazon's system, and you can find that at https://author.amazon.com. If you're a brand-new author, check that link after your book comes out.

In case you have no idea what I'm talking about, I mean this:

FUNNY YOU SHOULD ASK: HOW TO MARKET A BOOK 65

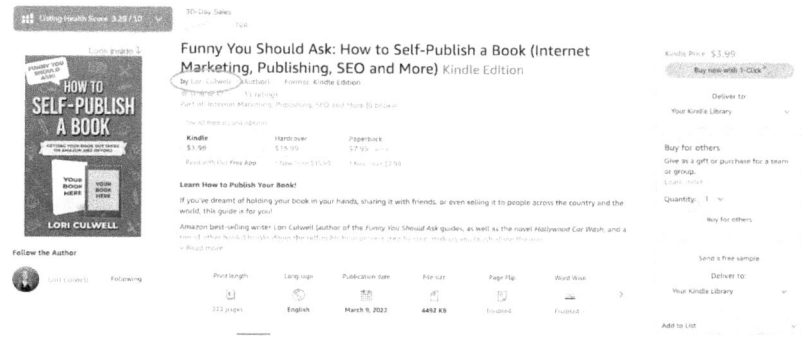

Which, when you click my name, takes you over to my Amazon Author profile:

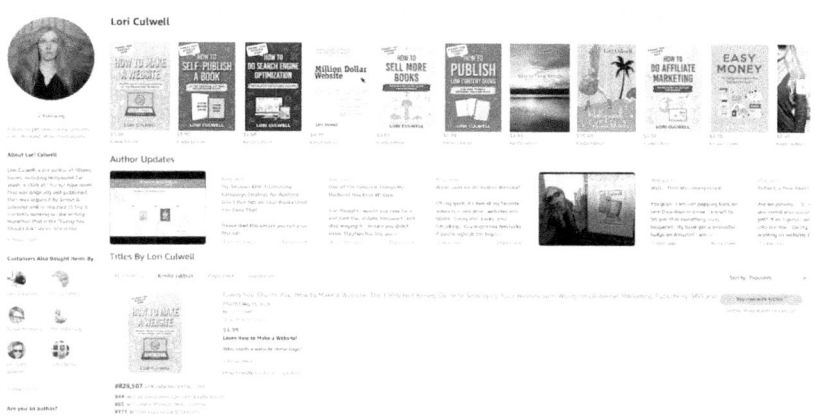

This is my profile, on which you can find photos of me, links to all of my books, and feeds from my various websites and social media. I've also written my website and social media links into my bio, just in case someone wants to find me over there.

• • •

If you don't fill out your Author Central profile, it will look like this, and that's just a big dumb waste of valuable Amazon space:

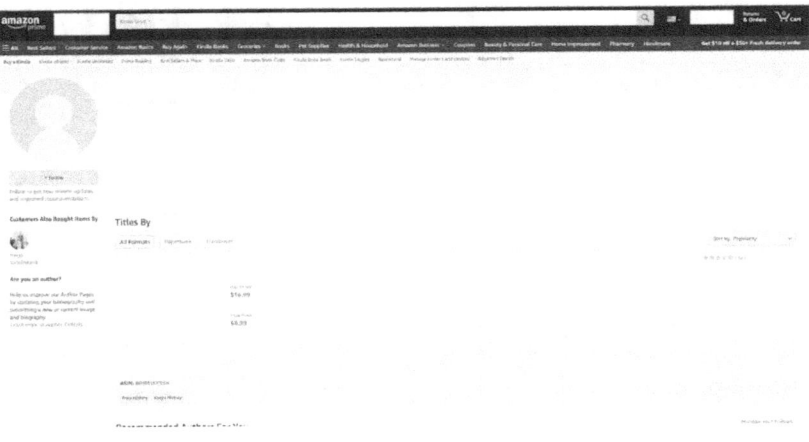

Come on! Your Amazon Author Central profile is your place on Amazon to put all of your books in one place and tell readers more about yourself as an author. It has to be set up properly, so let's get on that!

First, click "Edit Profile," then go back to your trusty author marketing folder and add all of the photos of yourself and any videos or book trailers you might have. Then go over to the bio section and fill that out, being sure to include references to your author website and social media where you are actually active. Amazon won't let you put actual links in your bio, but that shouldn't stop you from putting them in there. Every little bit helps!

. . .

Next, click the "Manage Blog Feeds" button, where you'll see this:

Blog Feeds		Status	Last updated	Add new feed

This is where you'll put the RSS feeds for your website so everything you post on your blog will appear on your Author Central page, making you look awesome and super organized (and giving people the chance to follow those links and hopefully get on your list). This is the only example I can find of Amazon actually linking back to an external source, and it's great for the SEO power of your author website because it provides automated, high-quality backlinks, but as I'm writing this I realize that I am the only one that is excited about such a thing, so I won't elaborate. Please take my word on this and put your website's RSS feed in there.

Be sure to also create an RSS feed for whatever social media you're most active on (using https://rss.app/). Click "Add new feed," and enter that as well. There is a remote chance you might pick up followers on social media this way, and we want to take every chance Amazon gives us.

Next, click on "Books." Hopefully, Amazon will have pulled all of your books into your library automatically, but if not, click the "Add it now" link to search for them on Amazon. You'll need to add them one at a time, which is annoying. Your books will be displayed in order of their popularity within Amazon, and you can't rearrange them, in case you're curious. I asked so you wouldn't have to!

. . .

That's all we can do for now on Amazon Author Central, but write yourself a note to update this in the future with any photos or videos pertaining to your fabulous author career. Any and all successes should be highlighted on this page, because you never know who might be clicking that link on your book listing!

Speaking of links, copy the link for your Amazon Author Central profile and put that in your "My Links" spreadsheet. While you have that spreadsheet out, go ahead and copy and paste all the links of all the different iterations of your books on Amazon: Kindle eBook, paperback, and hardcover. Each one has a different link!

Keep your promo stuff out, because next we're moving on to Goodreads. Amazon owns them, but of course they have a totally separate profile for you that you need to maintain, because automatically updating your profile from your Author Central would be way too simple. GoodReads also counts as social media and you can get in there and engage as much as you want on a social level. Right now we're just talking about setting your profile up properly so you don't miss any potential readers who might want to get on your list.

GoodReads (www.goodreads.com)

Storytime: In 2007 I was at a charity luncheon, seated next to a person who said she worked at GoodReads. I had just self-published a novel and proceeded to tell her all about how difficult it was to update books (especially book covers) in the GoodReads system, and to opine that if the people that started GoodReads were really that into books and authors, they would figure out a way to make this easier, because WTF.

I'm sure you can see where this is headed, and you're probably already cringing on my behalf.

This person graciously listened to me rant about this for ten minutes, then informed me that in fact *she* was one of the founders of GoodReads, and that she would "let the team know." That was an embarrassing and awkward moment for me, but they improved the "update book" functionality after that, so I guess… you're welcome?

The GoodReads Author Program

You're probably already on GoodReads (or you at least know about it), but if not, let's start from the beginning. Go over there and create an account, or log in and reset your password (if you're like me and have a million-year old profile that needs to be updated).

Pro tip: when they ask you (and oh boy, will they ask you) to "add friends" on Goodreads by connecting your Facebook or Gmail accounts, please say no. What you do not need is Amazon knowing all about who your friends are. When those friends go to leave reviews on your books, their reviews are unlikely to stick because Amazon now knows those people know you and technically "friends and family" reviews violate their terms of service. It's a trap!

GoodReads is primarily a reader-focused social media platform focused on book discussions and reviews, so you'll need to go the extra mile to set yourself up properly as an author. Here's the basic Goodreads setup for authors:

1. Find your books and claim your author page. Unlike Amazon where you are the default owner, Goodreads owns and controls any page not claimed by you. To get started with claiming your profile, search for one of your books, click your author name, then scroll all the way down to the bottom of the page, and click this (somewhat hard-to-find) link:

Is this you? Let us know.

Well, go ahead! Let them know!

Fill out the form and application, and once they've "verified" you (this can take up to two business days), you will be labeled a "Goodreads Author" and you'll have control of the page. Repeat this process for each and every one of your pen names.

Here's a slight conundrum: if your book just came out, it can take a little while for Goodreads to learn about it. You can't add a book manually unless you're already a verified Goodreads Author, and you can't become a Goodreads verified author unless you have a book.

So there's that. Just keep checking back and searching for the book until it appears in there. It doesn't actually take that long now that Amazon owns GoodReads (or maybe it changed because of my awkward charity luncheon rant. You don't know!)

Your books will hopefully all be visible on your profile because you will have selected them as part of the "Becoming a Goodreads Author" process, so just make sure those all look right.

. . .

2. Go to "edit author profile" and completely fill it out. Add your photo and bio, links to your author website and social media, the RSS feed from your blog, your interests, what kind of books you like to read, and the genre in which you write. Change the URL of your profile to reflect your actual name (because when you do that it will get picked up by Google and count as one of your "reputation management" slots).

3. Add the book to your own Goodreads "shelves," but do not give them star ratings. Shelves are divided into "to read," "reading," and "read."

4. Add your book to one or more lists (search on https://www.goodreads.com/list). And while you might have just thought "Oh cool, I'll just make a list called "Bestselling Books" and add my own books to that list," you would be incorrect because you can't add your own books to a list you created yourself. Take it from me!

That is all I would do for the setup, and you'll then need to decide whether Goodreads is going to be part of your book promotion and marketing life. If you're already using Goodreads as a reader (and therefore know the interface), it might be a good fit for you! Goodreads is widely regarded as one of the most successful social media platforms for authors, so definitely look around and see if it's something you want to pursue.

If you want to learn more about how to promote your books using GoodReads, I've put together some additional resources over at: https://bookpromotion.com/goodreads

. . .

BookBub (www.bookbub.com)

Next on the list of book-related sites where you definitely need to have a presence (or to claim and control the presence that you already have) is BookBub. We're addressing them now because they are going to come up later when we talk about paid promotional emails and I want you to already have a profile over there in case you want to apply for one.

You've probably already heard of BookBub, but if not, they are currently the 800-pound gorilla in the "free and discounted" book space, with something like 10 million people on their collective email lists and a ton of website traffic. BookBub is used by major traditional publishers for their book launches, so it's pretty hard to get them to pick your book if you're an indie author (and it's spendy if they do). But since they already know about you, you're better off just going over there and cleaning up your profile in case you want to pitch them one of your books in the future.

First, sign up as a reader, because it will help you to see what kinds of books they highlight in their famous promotional emails.

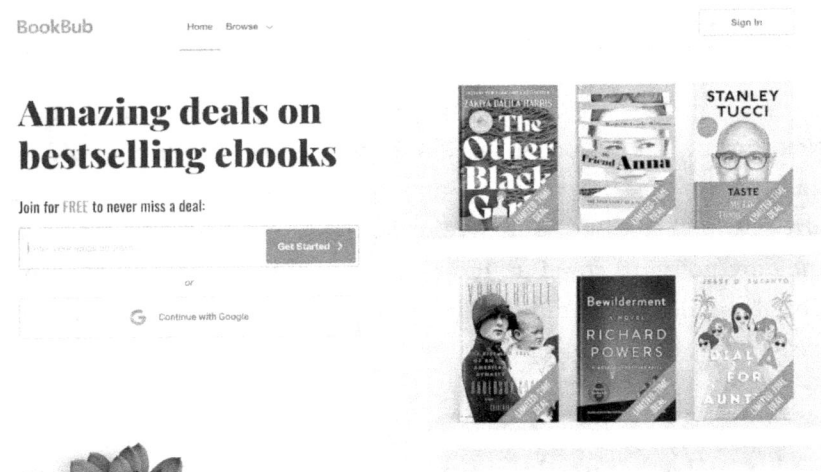

You will start receiving a daily email from BookBub, and I would love for you to just open that email every day so you can get a feel for the kinds of books they accept. It's also generally informative to look at a lot of book covers (especially those in your genre). What I'm saying is, you're trying to sell books, so make it a habit to regularly look at books that are selling. Start with the BookBub email.

Next, you'll need to sign up for a "partner" account at BookBub, which you can do at: https://partners.bookbub.com/. Once you've registered and started that account, you'll see this dashboard:

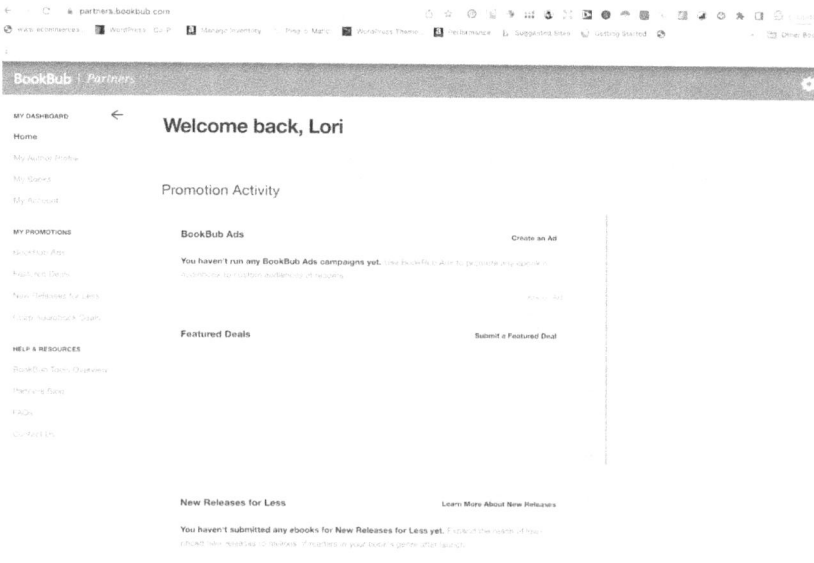

Right now we're just verifying and filling out profiles, so ignore all of the promotional things you can do on here and click "My Author Profile," where you will upload your photo, populate your bio, and put yourself into some genres. No possibility of linking to an author website or any social on BookBub (yet), so move on to the "My Books" tab, where some (probably not all) of your books will likely be represented. Whatever informational feed BookBub is pulling its book info from lags quite a bit (and by that I mean they didn't have any of my books published after 2010), so you'll need to search for your name or titles and add all of your books so they appear in your BookBub profile, like this:

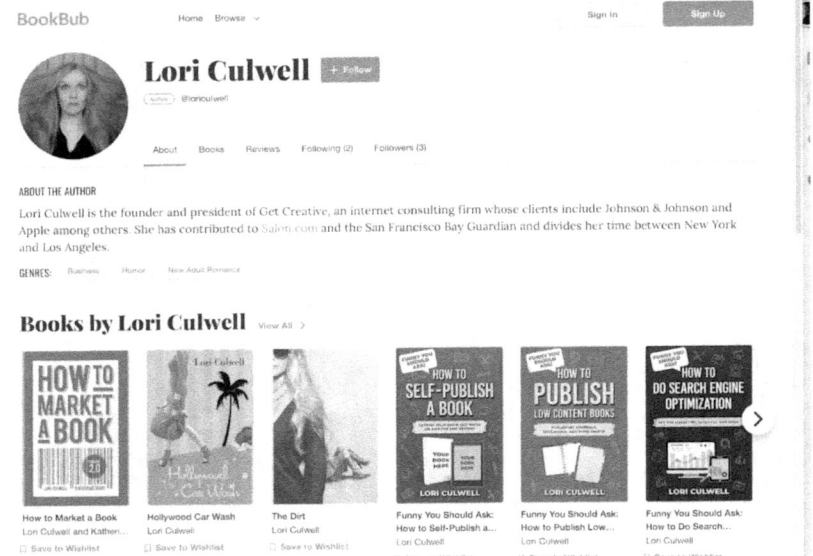

The intention here is to look like a real person (which you are) on BookBub, which is a good idea for several reasons: For one, you want some of the millions of people who subscribe to BookBub to "follow" you, because BookBub will notify those people when you release a new book. I don't know about you, but I will take all the free notifications I can get from anyone who is giving them out. When you get to 1,000 followers on BookBub, you gain the ability to promote a new book using a "pre-order alert," which is cool.

The other reason you want your BookBub profile up and running is so you can apply for some BookBub promotional deals, which we're going to talk about later in Chapter 15. You do not want to still be setting all of this up by then, because that will go on the list of "things that are never going to happen because you have "f*cking HAD IT with book promotion and marketing."

. . .

That was a real quote from a real author I recently worked with.

One Last Thing!

You're done with BookBub for now, so I will just leave you with one final task in the setup process: pulling all of this together with LinkTree. You'll want to give people the opportunity to consume your content or buy your books on the sites where they are most comfortable, so giving them choices is key. Grab that "My Links" spreadsheet from Chapter 2 (which I know you've been updating this whole time), and let's pull all of your hard work together into one organized link tree.

If you don't have one already, go over and start a LinkTree account at https://linktr.ee/. You're fine with a free account (at least initially). Next, populate your LinkTree with:

—your author website
    —links to any social media accounts on which you're going to actually be active
    —your Amazon author central link
    —your GoodReads profile
    —a link to sign up for your email list
    —a link to the "Press" section on your website (if traditional media is important to you)

What you'll put in your LinkTree should be informed by what you're planning on doing in terms of social media, as well as what outcomes you're looking to create (book sales, media interviews, email signups, etc.).

. . .

Once you have that final LinkTree link, put it in all of your social media profiles, in the signature box on your email, and anywhere else you think people might find you! Oh, and always remember to update your spreadsheets with all of your links and logins. The more organized you are, the easier it is for success to come your way.

Great job! Now that we have your author life performing like a well-oiled machine, let's turn our attention to your actual books!

PART 2: SEO FOR BOOKS

You've tackled the most important part of the long-term growth process— the arduous setup of the list and author platform. Keep up with that, and every single launch will be easier than the last.

We're now going to turn our attention to your current book and start preparing it to be found by potential customers.

Ideally you will do this research before you start writing your book so you can tailor it to perform competitively. This is also called "writing to market," which is a term you might have heard floating around in the indie publishing world.

This leads us to one of my favorite concepts, which is....Amazon is nothing but a big search engine filled with buyers, and to be successful authors we must accept this fact and act accordingly. Basically, we need to start treating our book listings like little websites and optimizing them so they will show up in the Amazon search rankings.

We're doing a ton of research in this module, going in-depth into your genre/ subgenre, your categories, your keywords, and your book's competition so we can take all of that information and optimize your book's listing for success. Going forward, we want your book to sell itself through organic traffic you get from Amazon searches, and for that, we need the help of the almighty Amazon algorithm.

Let's get going!

8

AMAZON IS A SEARCH ENGINE FOR BUYERS

I hope you're excited, because we're jumping right in with the nerdy talk here. I'm just about to start talking about marketing-type stuff like ranking and metadata now, so I'm taking off my author hat and putting on the one that says "website expert" for a moment. I'm hoping this example will help you get your head around what I'm trying to do with this section of the book. I come to this discussion from the unique perspective of having written and published a bunch of books while at the same time ranking websites in Google for about 20 years.

I'm talking like a website person for a second because I need you to start thinking about Amazon in a totally different way, like right now. You need to have an "aha" moment before I go all the way into the SEO nerd rabbit hole, because I don't want to lose you when I start talking about my love for keyword and category research and competitive analyses. This is all for your benefit! I swear!

. . .

First, let's agree that Amazon is now one of the world's most powerful search engines. In fact, it might be the most powerful one (sorry, Google!) because almost all of the traffic within Amazon is qualified buyer traffic, meaning most of the people who are searching for things on Amazon have their credit cards out and are looking to buy something.

Are we good? Amazon is a search engine for buyers? OK, good. I'm glad you're with me. To further verify this for yourself, think about your own behavior on Amazon. You go there with a list of things you want, type a few words into the search bar at the top, and boom! Amazon shows you what they think the best match is for each query. In fact, it is even copying Google and doing the auto-complete thing now, trying to suggest a bunch of variations of what you might be searching for!

That looks like this:

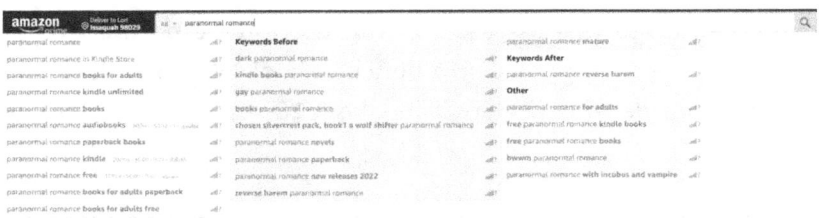

When you really stop and think about it, isn't this the exact same way you find things on Google? You type in what you want. What you type in is the "demand," and the Google results are the "supply" to meet that demand. Google is smart and wants you to keep coming back, so if you type in "best barbeque tools," it's not going to show you a website about koi fish.

Amazon is just like that, only the stakes are even higher because it knows you are sitting there wanting to actually buy something right then. In this example, paranormal romance is the demand, and all the books that come up are the supply.

Here's our challenge: we need to get your book to show up for words that people are actually searching for. For that to happen, we need to actually tell Amazon those words, then "train" the algorithm to show your book when people type in those words. We do that by properly optimizing your book's listing, which means putting those important keywords in key places on the backend. I'm guessing your book is probably not optimized for its keywords, so it is not triggering the algorithm when people search for those words, and that is part of the reason it is not selling. In other words: Amazon does not know what your book is about, so it is not showing it when people search for books like that.

If your book is live right now, it is probably only optimized for its own title and your author name, and unless you're already a famous author, I'm sorry to tell you this, but **no one is searching for your name or the title of your book.** If you're like 99% of authors I talk to, you didn't do any keyword research (because you didn't know you needed to) so you didn't take the opportunity to educate Amazon about your book.

This is that lightbulb moment: Amazon is not just going to "figure out" what your book is about. You need to take all the words that pertain to the genre/ category/ subject and use them to optimize your book's metadata. This sounds counterintuitive because it seems like Amazon should just figure this out automatically, but that is not the case. You need to do your own research and figure out your ideal keywords, then use your title, subtitle, and the seven keyword boxes to actually tell Amazon what words to show your book for. That way they can use your book to fulfill the need expressed when people type what they want into that search box or go looking in their favorite categories for what's new and noteworthy.

Here's what needs to happen with your book: people need to be able to **find it**, they need to **read it** (either through buying it or downloading it via Kindle Unlimited if you're participating in that), and they need to **like it**. When those three things happen for any given keyword or key phrase, that "teaches" Amazon's algorithm not only to keep showing your book for that search term, but to also add more keyword rankings to the mix to see if those are successful. Remember, all they want is to help their customers find the right book for their search.

Here's what each one of those factors means to us and how we (as authors) can control and influence them on our side:

"Find it" is your book showing up for the right keywords and categories on Amazon. You influence that by optimizing your book's listing properly, which means putting those words into your book's metadata (your title, subtitle, and seven keyword slots on the backend) and by putting your book into additional categories. You can't change your title or subtitle if your book is already published, but you can absolutely change the keywords and categories.

. . .

"Read it" is people liking the cover and the description enough to actually buy the book or download it. You influence that by performing a thorough competitive analysis and making sure your cover, price, and description are competitive with the books that are already being shown (ranking) for those terms.

"Like it" is people giving your book favorable ratings or reviews in an equal or higher number than the ratings and reviews of your competition. You influence that by hitting up your "street team" of superfans who leave reviews, by sending out advanced review copies to as many reviewers as you can find, and by participating in "promo stacks" to get your book out there when it launches. Ratings and reviews are like backlinks in Google, providing social proof and validation (both to the customers and to the Amazon algorithm). We'll get there a little later when we're done fixing your book's listing.

Wow! Looks like we've got our work cut out for us! The first thing we're going to do is a bunch of research, breaking your book down by genre, category, competition, and keywords, and I wanted to tell you upfront why we're doing that. Now you know!

A Note on the "Honeymoon Period"

I've covered all the other factors that go into Amazon's placement of your book except for one, which I have to address now.

. . .

The honeymoon period.

If you haven't launched your book yet, I have great news! In the first 15-30 days of any new book's life, Amazon pushes new books out for their chosen keywords to see how those books perform for everything I just covered. Since you're reading this before you publish your book, you should be able to go back and make changes based on the competitive analysis you are about to perform, then properly optimize your listing for the keywords you are going to research. This combination will hopefully get your book enough traction in its first 15-30 days to earn it a permanent place in the Amazon search results. Once that happens, you will start getting a certain amount of sales on autopilot, and you'll pick up new subscribers for free through the lead magnet in your book.

If you already launched your book, I have less-than-great news: You didn't know to do any of this, so Amazon pushed out your book during its first 15-30 days with no keywords. You didn't have an email list and you didn't know how to get reviews, so you maybe got a few from friends and family and then gave up. Your honeymoon period passed with lackluster results, so Amazon buried your book somewhere in its catalog and now you need a spelunking helmet with a light on it to find that sucker.

This is totally unfair to you (and your book), but there is a way forward. Go through the rest of this guide and make every improvement possible, then run paid advertising on the book to artificially replicate the honeymoon period. Even if you don't choose to do the "paid ads," part I would still recommend going through all of the research and optimization steps to give your book the fighting chance it never got. Learn this whole process, then apply all of it to your next book!

And with that, let's dive in and start doing some analysis and brainstorming!

9
KNOW YOUR GENRE/ SUBGENRE/ TROPES/ PEERS

F inally! Let's talk about your book!

Since our goal is to end up with a list of search terms that will bring up your book whenever someone enters them into Amazon, let's start with your book's genre, subgenre, and tropes. In other words, what is your book about?

I feel like this might be one of those "No duh, Culwell" moments, but I've found that authors sometimes assume everyone knows what their book is about and they forget to say the actual words. This happens all the time with people and their websites, so it is no surprise that it also happens with books. With that in mind, the very first thing you'll need to do is to make sure you are 100% clear on the exact genre or subgenre of your book, as well as any tropes you might use (if you write fiction). These are your first (and perhaps most important) keywords, and we need to identify them right now.

What I mean is this: If you write fiction, you don't just write novels. You write "steampunk dystopian romance," or "vampire thrillers," or "cozy culinary mysteries." Your main character is not just a person. They are a millionaire, or a billionaire, or a single dad, or a detective grandma. The more specific about all of this you can be, the better your books will do in Amazon's algorithm. Your keyword list should include all of the words you might assume are obvious. In fact, the more obvious the better!

This also applies to you if you write non-fiction. What problem are you solving, and how are you solving that problem in a unique way? With this book, I would say I am bringing you a hilariously detailed approach to book marketing and promotion that is going to help you sell more books. I cover a lot of topics in this book, including email marketing, author websites, keyword research, category research, and launch strategy, and my angle is that I do it in a (hopefully) funny way. That's a pretty good list of keywords right there!

I bring this up because of an interesting discussion I had recently in (where else?) a self-publishing Facebook group. It proved the point that authors often overlook the need to think about their keywords. Here's how it went:

Author: Here is the cover for my latest book. Why is it not selling?

. . .

Everyone: This cover is very generic. What is your genre?

Author: Adult fantasy.

Everyone: Please be more specific. Adult fantasy is a category, not a genre.

Author: Huh?

I won't bore you with the rest of what turned out to be a 100-comment-long discussion with the author getting extremely defensive. As it turned out, she had written a first-in-series romance novel about the adventures of a polyamorous merman, but her cover looked like something out of "Game of Thrones," so no one could tell what the book was actually about.

In case you think I'm glossing over what you just read, let me repeat it for emphasis: A POLYAMOROUS MERMAN. I think we can agree, that's a bit more… specific than "adult fantasy." Put that book into "adult fantasy," and it will be like a merman that gets swallowed up by a sea of competitors, never to be heard from again.

See what I did there? This is why you buy my books instead of those generic how-to guides. I'm HILARIOUS.

. . .

"Adult fantasy," by the way, has 100,000 competitive titles in the Amazon search results, so even AMAZON considers that to be too general a term.

Here's what scares me about a discussion like this. If the author bothered to do a competitive analysis at all, she most likely did one in the super-general category of "adult fantasy." She then gave those comps to her poor cover designer, who then had no choice but to make something super generic.

You see the problem.

By not being specific enough with her genre (or even being able to state what her book was actually about), this author wasted a lot of time and money on a cover that absolutely needs to be re-done. Unfortunately, the whole discussion got erased so I didn't get a chance to ask if she had also done her keyword and category research based on "adult fantasy." If she had, that'll all need to be redone as well.

Let's be clear. Am I saying this author needs to put her book under "Merman Polyamory"? No, I am not. That would actually be TOO specific, and would fall under the same "overly specific keywords" warning as "over-optimizing your metadata for your own name or the title of your book." A search phrase that specific is going to have a really low search volume, so it's not going to help you to get that specific.

. . .

I don't know a ton about this genre (and I know I'm not looking to get into a debate about whether a merman is a mammal or not), but if I were hired to work on this book, I would probably start my research a few levels below "adult fantasy," asking the author questions about the actual subject matter of the book until I got to something like "paranormal romance." Depending on whether the merman stays a merman or turns back into an actual man at certain points, we might also throw the term "shifter" onto the list. Is the merman gay? Are the adventures only under the sea, or do they also end up in Europe or Asia at some point? What else happens in the book? Is there mystery involved in the adventures? Does the story take place in the present, past, or future? Is there a shipwreck? These are the sorts of things you need to make sure Amazon knows about your book, because that's how prospective readers will find it.

My point is this: before you put your book out (or at least before you put your marketing plan together), spend some time poking around on Amazon until you figure out the perfect genre and subgenre for your book. Only then should you do your competitive analysis.

In the very next chapter, I will demonstrate a thorough competitive analysis that yields an absolute ton of useful information. But like I just said, I can't even START a good competitive analysis unless I know the genre and subgenre for the book.

If you're not quite sure where to start, go look at some of Amazon's browse categories: https://bookpromotion.com/categories

. . .

Once you've nailed down your genre and subgenre, repeat the exercise for all of the tropes you're using in the book. Think generalities and stereotypes for the people, things, and situations that appear in your book, and put them on the list: millionaire; grandma detective; single mom; gay best friend, merman, etc.

In closing, if we've learned nothing else here, please remember: Don't toss your merman into a sea of adult fantasy where he will be forever swept under the waves of the Amazon algorithm.

Moving on.

10
YOUR COMPETITIVE ANALYSIS

Look at us! We're already on a roll! You've identified your genre/subgenre/tropes and have put those on your keyword list. Great! That gives us a jumping-off point for some really interesting research. I am a "knowledge is power" kind of person and I want you to start feeling empowered as soon as possible, so let's start by taking a look at your competition to see what they are doing right (and wrong).

Here's what we're doing: back in the olden days of traditional publishing, you'd write your book proposal before you wrote your entire book (for non-fiction, at least. For fiction you'd often just write the entire book and send that in with your proposal, and that was terrible in a whole different way). Your *proposal* would include a full breakdown of the book's contents, a summary of each chapter, a section on your target audience (who would buy your book), a section on marketing (your plan to get your book to its audience), and then the all-important competitive analysis section. This is where you would name and discuss the most successful books already on the market (your competition), then make the argument as to how your book would differ from those popular books and ultimately be more successful than all of them (combined). The competitive analysis was where you would prove that you understood what was already working and that you knew what you had to "beat," so to speak.

This analysis is one of the tools I have brought over with me from traditional publishing, and I don't know why more people don't do it, especially in indie publishing where the competition is so fierce and you have to be so keenly aware of what is already working so you don't have to reinvent the wheel. I do this for all of my own books as well as every book I work on, because it saves me a ton of time and gives me a picture of what I need to do, marketing-wise. What I'm saying is, look to others who have gone before you to give you clues as to what you need to do. The answers are all there, right on page one of Amazon for your keywords!

It should be no problem for you to find some competitors for your book, especially if you're already a fan of your niche or genre. You've probably even read a few of your competitors' books, or you've at least seen them floating around in your Amazon searches, and you probably also have a good idea of your peers and other people who are writing books in this genre or category. Don't we all know the heavy hitters in our chosen genre? I certainly do!

If you have no idea what I'm talking about or where to even start with this, just go over to Amazon and type the genre or subgenre you came up with in the last chapter into the search bar. Because I like to amuse myself with theoretical examples, I am going to conduct a competitive analysis of a genre I just learned about while I was working on that last chapter: paranormal shifter romance. If you have written a novel (or a whole series!) in this genre, this is your lucky day, because I conducted a lengthy analysis of the 48 titles that appeared on Page One of Amazon search results for that term at the beginning of May, and I am about to outline exactly what I would do to market that type of book.

If paranormal shifter romance isn't your thing, this is also your lucky day, because this analysis was time-consuming and I have now read a lot of weird book blurbs, so this section is pretty funny.

Also, just to clarify— this example does not pertain directly to the polyamorous merman book, because I never heard back from that author as to whether her merman could turn back into a human man, so I don't know whether he is a "shifter" or not, okay? THESE DETAILS ARE SUPER IMPORTANT WHEN IT COMES TO MARKETING YOUR BOOK.

Here's what comes up when I type "paranormal shifter romance" into Amazon. I will let you take a look at these for a moment, then I'll start breaking down what I see and why I think they are ranked so highly and selling so well. Your competitive analysis is your opportunity to play amateur detective and critique other people's book marketing strategies.

The Alpha's Silent Mate: A Shifter Paranormal Romance
by Eve Bale
★★★★☆ - 5
Kindle
$0⁰⁰ kindleunlimited
Included with your Kindle Unlimited membership Learn More
Available instantly
Or $2.99 to buy

#3,909 in Kindle Store (Top 100)
#28 in Contemporary Fantasy Fiction
#67 in New Adult & College Fantasy (Kindle Store)
#70 in Werewolves & Shifters Suspense

ASIN: B09ZVBJZG7

Price History   Keepa History

Next Door Dragon Daddy: A Paranormal Shifter Romance (Secret Shifters Next Door Book 1)
Book 1 of 2: Secret Shifters Next Door
★★★★☆ - 34
Kindle
$0⁰⁰ kindleunlimited
Included with your Kindle Unlimited membership Learn More
Available instantly
Or $4.99 to buy

#768 in Kindle Store (Top 100)
#11 in Women's Fantasy Fiction
#20 in Werewolves & Shifters Suspense
#25 in Women's Action & Adventure Fiction

ASIN: B09SF8T3GC

Price History   Keepa History

Shift: A Dark Paranormal Shifter Romance (The Black Mountain Pack Book 1)
Book 1 of 2: The Black Mountain Pack
★★★★☆ - 179
Kindle
$4⁹⁹ $23.99
Available instantly
Other formats: Paperback, Hardcover

#103,736 in Kindle Store (Top 100)
#3,461 in Paranormal Werewolves & Shifters Romance
#4,356 in Werewolf & Shifter Romance
#5,983 in New Adult & College Romance (Books)

ASIN: B09Q8LBLHV

Price History   Keepa History

Fated Mates: Book 1 of the True Mates Series: A Werewolf Shifter Paranormal Romance
Book 1 of 8: True Mates
★★★★☆ - 1,424
Kindle
$0⁰⁰ kindleunlimited
Included with your Kindle Unlimited membership Learn More
Available instantly
Or $3.99 to buy
Other format: Paperback

#2,501 in Kindle Store (Top 100)
#2 in Paranormal
#16 in Mystery & Suspense
#42 in Werewolves & Shifters Suspense

ASIN: B01KECQ3DG

Price History   Keepa History

Night Hunter: A Paranormal Romance With Fangs! (Shifter Days, Vampire Nights & Demons In between Book 5)
Book 5 of 7: Shifter Days, Vampire Nights & Demons In between
★★★★☆ - 3
Kindle
$2⁹⁹
Available instantly
Other format: Paperback

#501,140 in Kindle Store (Top 100)
#1,129 in Vampire Thrillers
#1,625 in Vampire Suspense
#4,701 in Paranormal Demons & Devils Romance

ASIN: B09VY7N187

Price History   Keepa History

Cocky Alpha Shifters: A Shapeshifter Paranormal Romance & Urban Fantasy Anthology (Shifters Unleashed)
Part of: Shifters Unleashed (8 Books)
★★★★☆ - 22
Kindle
$0⁰⁰ kindleunlimited
Included with your Kindle Unlimited membership Learn More
Available instantly
Or $3.99 to buy

#163,024 in Kindle Store (Top 100)
#305 in Science Fiction Anthologies (Kindle Store)
#405 in Fantasy Anthologies & Short Stories (Kindle Store)
#1,561 in Dragons & Mythical Creatures Fantasy (Kindle Store)

ASIN: B09KHJ7L5T

Price History   Keepa History

Midlife Tiger's Last Chance: Tiger Shifter Paranormal Romance (Midlife Shifters Series Book 5)
Book 5 of 5: Midlife Shifters Series
Kindle Edition
$0⁰⁰ kindleunlimited
Included with your Kindle Unlimited membership on release date Learn More
This title will be released on March 10, 2023.
Or $3.99 to buy

#65,947 in Kindle Store (Top 100)
#916 in Paranormal Ghost Romance
#1,048 in Psychic Romance
#1,345 in Paranormal Demons & Devils Romance

ASIN: B09ZVGD1VG

Price History   Keepa History

Tempting the Wild Wolf: Shapeshifter Romance (Seneca...
Book 1 of 5: Seneca Falls Shifters
★★★★☆ ~ 255
Kindle
$0⁰⁰ unlimited
Included with your Kindle Unlimited membership Learn More
Available instantly
Or $3.99 to buy
Other format: Paperback

#41,478 in Kindle Store (Top 100)
#1,727 in Paranormal Werewolves & Shifters Romance
#1,938 in Romantic Fantasy (Books)
#2,077 in Werewolf & Shifter Romance

ASIN: B0792BQLF8

Price History   Keepa History

Dragon's Pet: A Dragon Shifter Paranormal Romance (Dragon's...
Part of: Dragon's Mate (5 Books)
★★★★☆ ~ 4
Kindle
$0⁰⁰ unlimited
Included with your Kindle Unlimited membership Learn More
Available instantly
Or $2.99 to buy

#105,956 in Kindle Store (Top 100)
#3,520 in Paranormal Werewolves & Shifters Romance
#4,392 in Werewolf & Shifter Romance
#4,543 in Romantic Fantasy (Books)

ASIN: B09Z6WSR5F

Price History   Keepa History

Shift: A Dark Paranormal Shifter Romance (The Black Mountain...
Book 1 of 2: The Black Mountain Pack
★★★★☆ ~ 176
Kindle
$4⁹⁹ $23.99
Available instantly
Other formats: Paperback, Hardcover

#101,769 in Kindle Store (Top 100)
#3,428 in Paranormal Werewolves & Shifters Romance
#4,269 in Werewolf & Shifter Romance
#5,880 in New Adult & College Romance (Books)

ASIN: B09Q8LBLHV

Price History   Keepa History

Well! I don't know about you, but I feel like I've already learned a few things today. I actually clicked through and looked at all 48 books on page one of the Amazon search results (you're welcome), and here are some conclusions I can draw just from that (shall we say) illustrative experience:

— This is a great keyword with a ton of commercial potential if you can get Amazon to show your book for it, and I know that because all of the books Amazon is showing on the first page have very low BSRs (bestseller ranks). If you've never heard of sales rank (also called bestseller rank or BSR) before, welcome! This is how we discuss how well things are selling on Amazon. In the world of sales rank and BSR, lower is better, with number-one being the absolute best and the goal we're all striving for. To get your search results to look like mine with the BSR of each book showing in the main search results, you'll need a nifty (free) plugin called DS Amazon Quickview, which you can find at: https://bookpromotion.com/quickview

— The cover art in this genre is very high quality and photograph-based across the board, and over half of the covers feature guys with ripped abs. As you can see, the covers are all high-concept with models and art, so one thing you would need to do for sure is to invest money in a great cover that can match or beat these covers. Unless you're a professional designer, this is not a genre you're going to be able to break into with a DIY book cover. Just for fun, I also calculated the number of covers that had either blue or purple backgrounds, and that number was 60%. Fact: my job is weird.

—The "honeymoon period" is real. In case you thought I was kidding (or perhaps exaggerating) about the fact that Amazon aggressively pushes out newly-released books to see if they convert for their genre and keywords, think again! Twenty-seven of the forty-eight books on the first page of results were books that had been released in the prior 15-30 days. That's 56%! That leads me to my next conclusion, which is:

— This genre favors a rapid release strategy. From what I can see, this genre seems to favor series with a lot of books in them, often with one new release per month. If you are going to try to compete in this subgenre, is that a release velocity you can match and exceed? Personally, I've been trying to get a book out once a quarter, and even that is pushing it and I'm mad at myself most of the time for even making that schedule. Know yourself, is what I'm saying.

— In each and every one of these book listings, the *subtitle* contains some combination of the main keyword or key phrase, "paranormal shifter romance," for which that book will ideally be found. In case you were not aware of this when you published your book, the subtitle actually does not have to appear on the book cover, and in all of these cases, this field is being used strictly for search and discovery purposes. As I mentioned, you unfortunately can't change the subtitle of your book once it is published, but definitely use the subtitle this way in all of your books from now on.

— This is clearly a genre that requires a series to succeed. Good to know! 16% of the listings on page one are actually box sets. That's good news for you if you have a series of books but you never knew about the honeymoon period, because it gives you a brand-new way to enter the market.

— Almost all of these books got a ton of early reviews (meaning, reviews that came in during the honeymoon period) and a high review count overall. The reviews for these books start rolling in right away, which implies several things— these authors probably have street teams (or at least large email lists), have sent out a ton of ARCs (advanced reader copies) on social media and/or on services like BookSprout or BookSirens, and are likely participating in promotions (paid or free) to get their books out there. Case in point: the book on the far left had just come out (on May 10th, 2022) when I started this analysis and was accumulating reviews at the rate of approximately 5 per day, thanks to what was apparently a very successful BookSprout ARC campaign. If you're curious, search for that book on Amazon to see how many reviews they're up to now! (Note: I cover all of this ARC stuff in Chapter 14.)

— This genre favors (almost requires) enrollment in KDP Select so the books will be part of KU (Kindle Unlimited). Note that the BSR of "The Shift," which is the one book that is not available through KU, is significantly higher than the others. If you don't want to leave your book in KDP Select forever because you're going for a wider distribution strategy, that's fine, but it helps to at least put it in KDP Select for its first 90 days just to initially train the algorithm to show your books and amass reviews. Totally up to you!

— Pricing: For those books not enrolled in Kindle Unlimited, prices of these books range from $.99 - $5.99, with the largest number (13) being on the higher side at $4.99. That's good news for authors in this genre, because obviously, the more you can charge for your book, the better.

—Descriptions: Almost all of these books have excellent, keyword-focused descriptions with hooks that make you want to read the book.

That analysis took about an hour, and it only took that long because I clicked down into each listing to be thorough. As you can see, just that one analysis alone got me a ton of good info that I could use to successfully launch a book in that genre or for that keyword.

. . .

I want to acknowledge that the overwhelm factor is real with this exercise, because you've just learned about a ton of stuff that you never even knew you had to do and you might have just realized why your books have not been selling. It's okay! Take a deep breath! We'll take this step by step, I promise.

Here are the instructions for doing a competitive analysis for your book. First, you're going to take the keyword that best represents the genre or subgenre you figured out from the last chapter and type it into the Amazon search box.

You're going to be taking a bunch of notes for the genre itself and for each title, so I would recommend starting a new document (Word/Pages/Docs/whatever you use) because you're going to be referring to this throughout the entire process of marketing your book. Put it in the Book/Series Title folder you created in Chapter 3.

Here's everything you'll need to investigate and write down (or screenshot) for each of the 5-10 most popular books for this keyword, which represents your genre or subgenre:

1. What do the **covers** of these 5-10 books look like? You don't have to do an analysis of all 48 books on page one like I did (although it will really help you if you do!). Take a bunch of screenshots and stick all of those in the folder. You will be sharing them with your designer (or referring to them if you design the cover yourself). You're trying to get a feel for the dominant themes of the genre (like my guys-with-ripped-abs observation) and to give your designer (or yourself) some guidance so your cover design meets or exceeds the standard.

. . .

2. Are there any trends in the **descriptions** of your competitors that you can use for your book's description? Read the description of at least 5-10 of your top competitors. For fiction, are they all starting out strong with a hooky premise that grabs you and makes you want to find out what happens? For non-fiction, do they all have bullet points outlining what you'll learn in the book? Make sure your book has a description that follows the same patterns as the successful books while using your good keywords.

Side note: I am not saying to copy covers or descriptions. Don't come back and say I said that! Just make a note of what is working and apply those principles to your own book's listing if possible. Stealing is never the answer! Crime does not pay!

3. What is the average **price** of the top 5-10 competitive books? You need to price your book accordingly. Too low and you'll make people wonder about the quality of the book. Too high and you'll price yourself out of the market. You think this doesn't matter, but it is one of the first things I look at when troubleshooting a book. Oftentimes I will find that the price of the book in question is wildly out of step with its competition, and changing the price makes the book start selling. I hope this is your book's problem, because it is the easiest thing to fix!

4. How many **reviews** does each book have? This will let you know how difficult it might be to stay on the first page for that phrase after your book's honeymoon period has passed and will help you plan your launch. If every book that "sticks" on page one has 100 reviews, you'll need to build your street team, send out a ton of

advanced review copies (ARCs) prior to launch, or consider using a service like BookSprout or BookSirens. We'll cover reviews in the next section.

5. Speaking of reviews, go through and read your **competitors' one-star reviews**, not to laugh, but to learn. Make note of what people don't like about those books, and make absolutely sure that your book doesn't have any of those problems. Does that author really not understand the genre? Does the book have typos or grammatical errors? I know you'll do this anyway, but make sure you have a great proofreader in place to guarantee that doesn't happen. Every one-star review against a competitor is a magical window into what not to do, and you get this benefit without having to actually experience the one-star pain yourself. We haven't even talked about whether your book is any good yet (we'll get there), but if you already know it has problems, now is the time to address those.

Here's an example:

Cliffhanger
Reviewed in the United States on April 2, 2022
Verified Purchase

This is an excellent story... very engaging and well written... but suddenly stops in the middle of the plot, and a second book has to be purchased to reach a conclusion. I will not support authors who ambush their readers.

One person found this helpful

Ouch. So... don't do that. Make sure your book is high-quality, or no amount of promotion and marketing in the world is going to help you! I am a marketing expert, not a magician!

6. What **Amazon Browse Categories** are each book ranking for? Do not even worry if you don't know what browse categories are right now, because we're going to cover that topic at great length. Because you took my advice and installed that nifty DS Amazon Quickview plugin, you can see every book's sales rank and browse categories at once, like this:

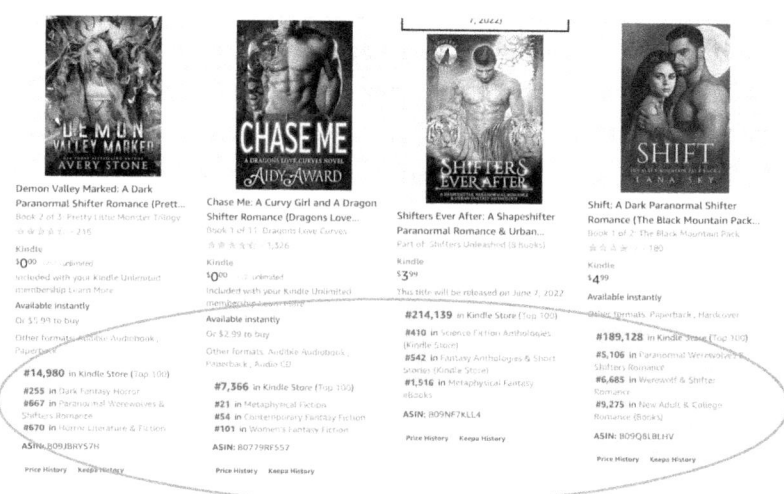

I'm psychic, so I hear you wondering: how did these authors get their books into those fantastic categories? How can you do that for your book? It might have happened organically for them, or they might have requested those categories (which is a thing you can totally do!). If you self-published your book, you picked two categories when you uploaded it. Those were BISAC categories, which are different from the categories Amazon puts your book into (more on this in the next chapter). What you might not know is this: you can research better categories and request that Amazon add your book to them, which can help people find the book and even earn you a bestseller badge! We're going right into category research in the very next chapter, but for now, write down any category you think might also be appropriate for your book. We are in "learning from other people's successes" mode right now.

. . .

7. Keyword research—what **keywords** does it seem like each book is optimized for? We will go much further down the keyword rabbit hole soon, but for now, just look at each listing and try to figure out what keywords the author wanted that book to be found for. Look in the metadata you can see—the title, subtitle, and description—and try to reverse-engineer from there. I'm telling you, it's like a game of I Spy for keywords, and once you see it, you'll never look at another book listing the same. If you see any keywords that pertain to your book, add those to your list, because this is proof that they are successful!

If you're already like "I don't have time to do any of this," I would highly recommend checking out Publisher Rocket (www.publisherrocket.com), which is paid software that lets you quickly do a lot of this in-depth analysis. Publisher Rocket is great, because it can also pull your keywords and categories for you. No pressure, though! You can totally do all of this by hand!

Great job! I'm sure your mind is positively overflowing with information and new ideas, so take a moment to organize your notes and screenshots. In the next chapter, we're jumping right into category research!

11

CATEGORY RESEARCH

Now that you know all about your competition, let's find you some great categories to put your book in so it will be found by even more potential fans.

Category research is another one of those "I never knew to do that" activities that you should always do before you put your book out but that you can also do at any time after your book is published to help its discoverability within Amazon. Believe it or not, people are still finding new books by clicking down into their favorite categories, and I know that because of the existence of the categories themselves. If categories didn't help people find books, Amazon would stop displaying them that way. Amazon wants to make money, so they don't do things just for show.

Categories are a whole world within Amazon, and surprise! That world is based on search keywords because Amazon is a search engine for buyers. Because they love to do everything their own way, Amazon has invented its own categorization system called "Browse Categories," with over 17,000 different sub-categories (as opposed to the approximately 4,000 BISAC categories of the traditional publishing industry, which is what you stuck your book into when you published it). In case you've never noticed this (and why would you, really?), books are displayed within Amazon by their BSR (bestsellers rank) within each Browse Category.

That looks like this:

> **Best Sellers Rank:** #413,187 in Books (See Top 100 in Books)
> #1,767 in Cognitive Psychology (Books)
> #51,076 in Self-Help (Books)
> **Customer Reviews:** ★★★★☆ ⌄ 25 ratings

The lowest (best) rank for this book is in the "Cognitive Psychology" browse category, where it is #1727. That's great and is certainly helping the book's overall visibility within Amazon, but what this author should do is dig deeper into category research to find a category so small and specific that its existing daily sales would make it #1. That way, when people who find books by browsing categories happen upon that category, that book will be sitting pretty in the #1 slot, complete with one of those cool orange bestseller badges.

Because really, isn't that why we all started writing in the first place? For the cool orange bestseller badge?

. . .

I'm kidding. Sort of. That's not *why* we do it, but it's a nice confidence booster when it happens, and it does end up helping your book sales. I say all of this from personal experience, because here is one of my books with the cool orange badge:

Whoa! Did that wake you up? Are you interested now? I know this subject matter is a little dry, so I like to put these little Easter eggs in here for you, just as a pattern interrupt.

Since I'm assuming I now have your full attention and you are super motivated to do this research, let's jump right in! You can achieve a similar result by digging down into the depths of all the categories and subcategories that are relevant to your genre/sub-genre until you find one that has a #1 bestseller (for that category or sub-category) that you know you can beat. You'll then ask Amazon to add you to these great categories, and eventually you'll get a cool orange badge of your very own. Because again, that's why we're writers.

. . .

Category Research: the Manual Method

First I will outline how to do your category research manually, which takes a long time and is a little aggravating. I'm telling you this because I want you to be able to do all of your book marketing on a shoestring budget if that's where you're at right now, so when I say "manually," please be aware that I mean "free" but "time-consuming." I personally use Publisher Rocket (a paid software) for this research, and I cover that later in this chapter.

Start your category research by going to the "Books" link in the Category sidebar. One by one, click on every category and subcategory that is remotely relevant to the genre/subgenre of your book. Put these categories into a spreadsheet. Be sure to also include the BSR (bestsellers rank) of the book that is #1 in that category, because you'll need it later to determine how many copies that book is selling per day.

The category sidebar looks like this. Don't be afraid. Just get in there and start clicking and recording BSRs.

FUNNY YOU SHOULD ASK: HOW TO MARKET A BOOK

Books
- Arts & Photography
- Biographies & Memoirs
- Books on CD
- Business & Money
- Calendars
- Children's Books
- Christian Books & Bibles
- Comics & Graphic Novels
- Computers & Technology
- Cookbooks, Food & Wine
- Crafts, Hobbies & Home
- Deals in Books
- Education & Teaching
- Engineering & Transportation
- Health, Fitness & Dieting
- History
- Humor & Entertainment
- Law
- Lesbian, Gay, Bisexual & Tra
- Libros en español
- Literature & Fiction
- Medical Books
- Mystery, Thriller & Suspense
- Parenting & Relationships
- Politics & Social Sciences
- Reference
- Religion & Spirituality
- Romance
- Science & Math
- Science Fiction & Fantasy
- Self-Help
- Sports & Outdoors
- Teens
- Test Preparation
- Textbooks
- Travel

‹ Books
Religion & Spirituality
- Agnosticism
- Atheism
- Buddhism
- Christian Books & Bibles
- Hinduism
- Islam
- Judaism
- Literature & Fiction
- New Age & Spirituality
- Occult & Paranormal
- Other Eastern Religions & Sacr
- Other Religions, Practices & Sa
- Religious
- Religious Studies
- Worship & Devotion

‹ Religion & Spirituality
New Age & Spirituality
- Angels & Spirit Guides
- Astrology
- Celtic
- Chakras
- Channeling
- Divination
- Dreams
- Druidism
- Gaia
- Goddesses
- Meditation
- Mental & Spiritual
- Mysticism
- New Age
- New Thought
- Reference
- Reincarnation
- Sacred Sexuality
- Shamanism
- Spiritualism
- Theosophy
- Urantia
- Wicca, Witchcraft & Paganism

‹ Books
‹ Religion & Spirituality
‹ New Age & Spirituality
Wicca, Witchcraft & Paganism
- Paganism
- Wicca
- Witchcraft

If you've never paid a lot of attention to categories and subcategories on Amazon, you are now a little shocked at just how hilariously granular Amazon gets with its categorization system. Like, has that always been there, and you've never noticed it? Weird!

. . .

Each subcategory is more specific and has fewer books in it than the one above it, making it easier to become a bestseller in there. This is your classic "big fish, small pond" scenario. Just keep looking until you find the pond where your book can be the biggest fish.

Keep going into each category, writing down each one you might want your book to go into until you have a decent-size list. Then click down into each to see the best-selling books. Next, take the BSR of the top books in each category and subcategory and run those through this excellent (and free) little tool (https://kindlepreneur.com/amazon-kdp-sales-rank-calculator/) to determine how many books per day those books are selling. That way, you'll know how many books per day *you'll* have to sell to get that orange badge. Put those numbers in the spreadsheet.

In case that was too much data flying at you at once and you are now inexplicably overwhelmed and maybe even a little bored, I will present this scenario to you again in story form. Say you have a book about gardening that you want to get selling a little better. I would initially point you toward a thorough competitive analysis so you could make sure your book was indeed competitive with the bestsellers for its subject matter. First we would make whatever improvements needed to be made to the cover, description, and reviews of your book. Then we would do some category research to see if we could get your book placed more favorably in Amazon's Browse Categories and maybe get it a bestseller badge to get it noticed when potential customers happen upon it while searching.

Here are the bestsellers in the "Gardening & Landscape Design" category:

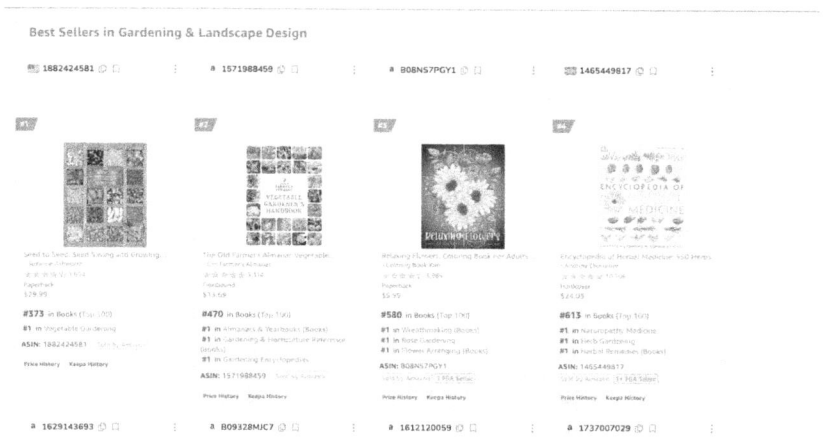

Just so you don't have to do math in your head, I will tell you that to be #1 in this category, you would need to sell 123 books per day.

That's probably going to be a little too ambitious for a first-time author who is only just starting their email list, so I would keep asking you questions about your book and researching categories based on your answers. As it turns out, all of the flowers you talk about are annuals, so we're putting your book into this category: **Books > Crafts, Hobbies & Home > Gardening & Landscape Design > Flowers > Annual**

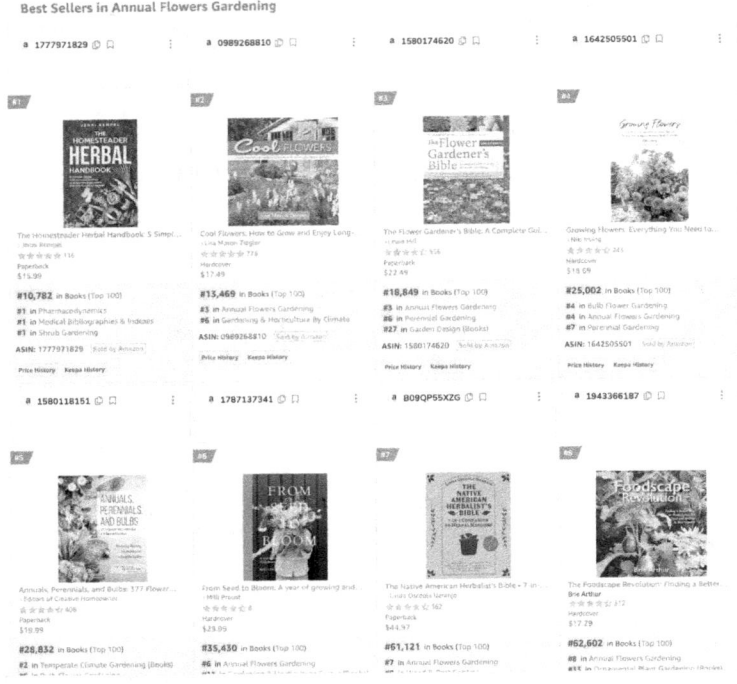

As you can see, the book that is ranked #1 for this category has an overall sales rank (meaning, in all of Books) of 10,782.

When I take that number and run it through the Sales Rank Calculator, I get this:

What this means is that to achieve #1 status in this much smaller and more specific category, this book is selling 15 books per day. Much more manageable! You can easily achieve that number with some paid advertising.

Obviously, the way to reverse-engineer this approach would be to determine how many books you think you can sell (based on your email list, social media followers, advertising budget, or whatever else you have going on), then find a category where you can be #1 with that number of sales. Same difference, sort of, but the first one leads with the subject matter while the second leads with numbers.

What you'll need to do is keep poking around until you find ten categories that a) only need a number of sales you think you can actually generate to be the #1 seller, and b) are actually relevant to your book.

Yes, I KNOW, even reading all of that was a lot, and I do not expect you to actually do all of that, but I did just want to describe the whole method in case you are in a place in your marketing journey where you have, let's say, more time than money. That's OK! There is a (much) faster way to conduct this research and come up with these favorable categories, but it does involve a paid tool, so I wanted to just give you the manual, free way to do it so you wouldn't feel like I was dangling some secret method in front of you that you could only get by paying. I am not that person!

The Paid Method

The (much, *much*) faster way to do this process is to pay for some cool software that will sift through all the categories for you and tell you where to put your book so that it can hit #1. This software is called Publisher Rocket, and it was created by a self-publishing and marketing genius named Dave Chesson. If you're able to, I think you should invest in it without delay, and if you know me at all, you know that I am not the kind of person who ever wants you to pay for something if I don't use it myself. I am totally serious about saving people money, so when I not only buy something myself but also endorse it, you know it has to be great.

Here's how Publisher Rocket solves the "which category should I pick?" problem. You type in a word, and Publisher Rocket searches all of the categories, giving you an estimate of how many books you would need to sell to get to the #1 slot:

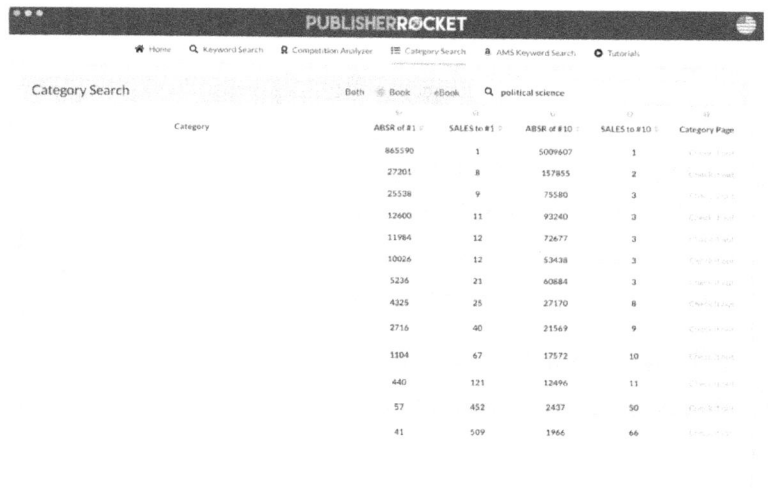

I have blurred out the categories Publisher Rocket came up with because that is their actual business and I respect them, but suffice it to say, it was flower-related.

I will say that Publisher Rocket is the one tool I think you absolutely cannot live without if you are trying to market books yourself, for this as well as many other reasons. It can also give you a list of keywords for you to put into the keyword slots, tell you what words to advertise against, and do your competitive analysis for you. That's going to save you a ton of time that you and I both know you do not want to be spending on book marketing.

My final argument for you to invest in Publisher Rocket is that I think you can use it to gain a competitive edge in many areas of self-publishing for a relatively small investment (it's like $97), which is going to really help you because many other people who self-publish want to get everything for free. (That's right, I said it.)

Oh, and one final word of warning: I know you've probably seen people doing this, but DO NOT, and I repeat, DO NOT EVEN THINK ABOUT intentionally putting your book into a category where it obviously does not belong just to try to get that bestseller badge. That was not the point of this chapter, and it's definitely not something you should do. Gaming the system like that is a blatant violation of Amazon's Terms of Service and is grounds for Amazon to terminate your KDP account. If you saw a video by some random YouTube "guru" telling you to do that, please ignore them. They are very wrong.

Once you get to ten good Browse Categories for your book, stick those in your book research folder, and let's move on to keyword research!

12

KEYWORD RESEARCH! MY FAVORITE!

It's time for my favorite thing—keyword research! If you're just about to publish your book and you need to add some keywords to those all-important seven keyword slots on Amazon, fantastic! If you didn't do that and you now have a book that needs some retroactive marketing help, it's never too late! Almost every time I talk to an author about my love for keyword research, they roll their eyes and assume this research is a cynical and overly-technical thing that marketers use to artificially force sales. I get how you could think that if you're brand new to marketing, but it's actually wrong and we need to get you past that assumption so your book can be successful.

Here's the thing: as I've now mentioned enough times to annoy you, Amazon is nothing but a search engine for buyers, and if you don't fill in your keyword information properly, Amazon's not going to know what your book is about and what to show it for. If it doesn't know, it can't help you make sales, and that pretty much guarantees the book is not going to take off organically. That's just common sense.

You've already got a good list going just based on your genre, subgenre, tropes, categories, and the keywords your competitors are using, so this is going to be a final sweep to make sure we have enough words to perfectly optimize your metadata.

And what do I mean by "metadata," exactly?

Technically, the metadata of your book includes your title, subtitle, keyword boxes, and description. If you haven't hit "Publish" on your book already, please try to fit your best keyword phrase into your title or subtitle, like the paranormal-shifter romance examples in the competitive analysis. This is absolutely an acceptable use of the subtitle space and something all indie authors should take advantage of.

If you have already published your book, you will not be able to change the title or subtitle, so you'll need to work with what you have: the keyword boxes and the description.

I'm talking about these keyword boxes, in case you didn't fill them out (or it's been a while and you've forgotten about them):

Here's the thing: I love Amazon, but they do a terrible job of explaining how to fill in these keyword slots and how important they are to the overall success of your book. When they say to choose up to seven keywords that describe your book, what they mean is "each of these slots holds up to 50 characters, which is a lot more than seven keywords, and also, these boxes are really not optional."

Because Amazon doesn't tell you this, I'M TELLING YOU. These are some of the primary pieces of information Amazon uses to not only rank your book for generic customer searches, but to put that book into the "Browse Categories" system that we discussed in the last chapter. You've gotta tell Amazon something about your book, and this is your direct line in to do just that.

Also, in case you are about to go fill up those spaces with "my keyword my keyword my keyword my keyword" just to complete this exercise, I will let you know that I have tested many different iterations of what to put in these boxes on over 3,000 books (not a typo!), and I have concluded that repeating words does no good at all, so I would recommend that you put different words (up to 50 characters) in each box. Make the most of this space!

So, where do you get the keywords? If you're already familiar with the keyword research process (because you make websites or do some other marketing thing) and have software that you like, great! Save yourself some money and use that. If you don't have a preference, I'm going to show you a couple of different ways to compile a solid list of keywords so you don't choke when you're staring down the barrel of the seven keyword slots. I use Publisher Rocket for this because I like the way they color-code the commercial potential of the various keywords, but I'm also going to show you a manual (free) way to build a keyword list.

You can start by going right on over to Amazon, typing in your main keyword, seeing what autocomplete keywords Amazon shows you, and using whatever is relevant to your book.

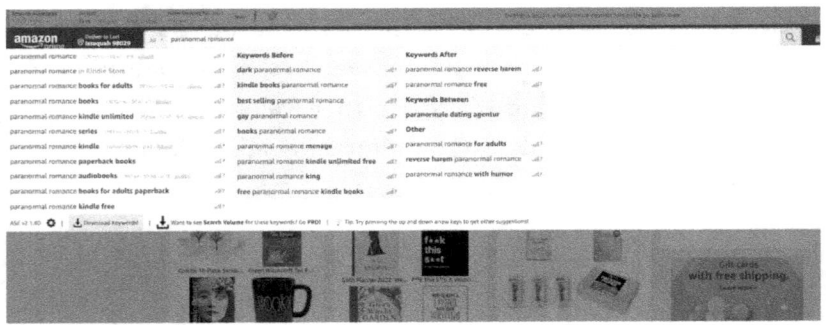

I have the free "AMZ Suggestion Expander" plugin installed to get these results, which you can find over at: https://loriculwell.com/amzsuggest

Add these words to your already-existing list that you have going. Then go through and answer all of these questions (use a pencil and paper if you want!), then save the answers to use when you're filling out the keyword boxes during the upload.

1. What kind of book is this? This is the "high level" genre/ subgenre/ trope question again. For fiction, you can use words like "fiction, series, paranormal, mystery," or whatever category/ genre you're publishing in. For non-fiction, I would start with "non-fiction," then go from there. Is it a book of essays? Is it a self-help book? Cookbook? Say something describing anything! You'll also want to use words indicating what kind of book this is, like "paperback, Kindle eBook, hardcover," etc.

2. What does your book have in it? This is your chance to describe the content of the book in keyword form. For our "paranormal fiction" example, we would put those words, then "vampire, werewolf, gnome, princess," and whatever other characters you might find in that book. For non-fiction, I would describe techniques, topics, tools, and anything else you cover. Did you write the definitive encyclopedia of cheese? Now is your chance to list all of the cheeses.

3. Who is most likely to read this book? This is a question for determining your target audience. Who did you write this book for? Your list might look like this: women, teens, moms, romance

lovers, girls, men, grandmas, etc. At first, all authors say "I want everyone to read my book," but eventually, we realize that not everyone's going to like what we're dishing out, so give this one some thought.

4. Why might someone buy this book? This is an "occasion" or context question. Your list might include: birthday gift, Christmas, education, textbook, self-help, and so on.

5. What keywords does it seem like your competitors' books are optimized for? You can usually tell if a book is optimized for keywords by looking at its subtitle.

Those were the "manual" methods of pulling keywords, and they will work just fine for a first-time publisher. If you're in a super competitive genre or you want to go much deeper into your keyword research, I have two paid suggestions for you. The first one is Helium10.

If you followed my "competitive analysis" instructions, you'll hopefully have a list of 5-10 books that you would consider your main competition. Your best move is to see what keywords those books are ranking for.

First, go over and sign up for a "starter" account at www.Helium10.com. This account is $29/ month and you can stop it or start it anytime you want, so most authors I know will turn it on for a month when they are about to launch a new book. Helium10 is an excellent research and analysis tool that is mostly used by people who sell physical products on Amazon, but it works great for books and publishing.

Once you've signed up, you're looking for a feature called "Cerebro," which is a nifty reverse search tool that will let you spy on your competitors' keywords.

To do your keyword research with Cerebro, you'll need to grab the ASIN of each book on your competitors' list. You can find that on each book's listing by scrolling down until you see this:

Product details

ASIN : B0779RF557
Publisher : Coffee Break Publishing (February 1, 2018)
Publication date : February 1, 2018
Language : English
File size : 1901 KB
Simultaneous device usage : Unlimited
Text-to-Speech : Enabled
Screen Reader : Supported
Enhanced typesetting : Enabled
X-Ray : Enabled
Word Wise : Enabled
Print length : 266 pages
Lending : Enabled
Best Sellers Rank: #6,737 in Kindle Store (See Top 100 in Kindle Store)
  #18 in Metaphysical Fiction
  #50 in Contemporary Fantasy Fiction
  #89 in Women's Fantasy Fiction

Customer Reviews: ☆☆☆☆☆   1,356 ratings

Click "Cerebro Reverse Product Lookup" in Helium10 and you'll see this screen:

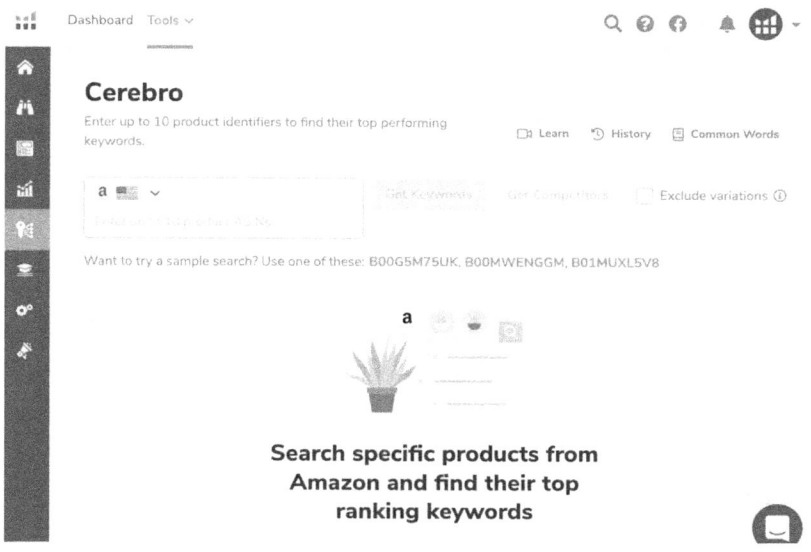

Take the ASIN of the first competitor and put it in the space. For this example, I'm doing a reverse search on my own book, "Funny You Should Ask: How to Self-Publish a Book" (which, yes, you should totally read if you haven't published your book yet).

My book is ranking for 246 keywords, which means that Amazon knows what the book is about and is serving it up when people type those keywords into the Amazon search bar. This is free publicity for my book, which I very much appreciate. Thanks, Amazon!

I obviously didn't put 246 keywords into the seven keyword slots (not because I didn't want to, but because that is impossible), so that means Amazon has taken the keywords I gave it,, mixed that with real people's search queries and buying habits, and is even testing keywords of its own.

If I scroll down a little bit, I can actually see all the keywords my book is ranking for, and here is a screenshot of that. I have blocked out the keywords because, a) I don't want to give away too much of Helium10's secret sauce, and b) those are my own book's keywords. Come on!

Keyword Phrase	Cerebro IQ Score	Search Volume	Search Volume Trend	Sponsored ASINs	Competing Products	CPR	Title Density	Match Type	Amazon Rec. Rank
	5	98	108%	140	>20,000	8	12	A	76
	3,936	984	106%	112	250	12	1	A	58
	36	362	102%	260	>10,000	8	13	A	60
	724	404	83%	249	682	9	3	S	
	111	222	79%	120	>2,000	8	2	A	20
	371	371	77%	213	>1,000	0	0	S	
	46,000	506	74%	31	11	9	2	A	90
	19,650	9,314	71%	247	474	37	6	A O	1
	46	137	71%	66	>3,000	8	1	S	
	7	27	71%	0	>4,000	8	12	A	39
	86	258	67%	309	>3,000	0	0	O	
	1,250	35	62%	0	28	0	0	A	52
	39	391	61%	234	>10,000	8	3	O	
	3,683	453	61%	134	123	0	0	A	121

Please note (important!): this is a confusing moment that can come back to bite you later, so I'm going to stop and explain it here. Some of the keywords you find during these searches are going to be the names of other authors and their books. That's all well and good, but it is NOT OK for you to intentionally put those words into the seven keyword slots. Catch-22 alert: It is okay for AMAZON to rank your book for these keywords and you might make sales based on people searching for those words and happening upon your book, but it is NOT OK for you to intentionally put these keywords in your metadata. DON'T DO THAT! That's a violation of the Terms of Service, and Amazon will definitely catch you doing that, and they will come after you. I did not say to do that! Don't say I said that!

For example, my book *is* ranking for the term "newsletter ninja," which is great for me because I love Tammi Lebrecque's books and I do think our audiences overlap, but *I did not put that title in my back-end keywords*, because, again, that goes against Amazon's terms for keywords and metadata. Amazon has determined that when customers type in "newsletter ninja," it might also be nice to offer them my book (yay!), but I did not do anything to cause that to happen.

Sorry for the semi-ranty sidebar, but I wanted to make sure you understood that you absolutely cannot put other people's names or book titles into your keyword slots. You're just looking for the *keywords and key phrases* for which Amazon is ranking your competitors' books with the intention of using those words in your book's metadata.

You'll repeat the reverse-search process for however many books you have in your "competitive titles" list, which should give you a list of about 25-30 keywords. If this is the method you're using, stick those keywords into an Excel spreadsheet, save them in the "Research" folder you made in Chapter 2, and you're done! Feel free to move on to the next chapter.

If you feel like that method is going to be too time-consuming, another (possibly better) way to do the keyword research for your books is to use Publisher Rocket, which you can get at https://publisherrocket.com

To pull keywords using Publisher Rocket, you would just start with a general keyword or phrase, then the software does the rest.

I started with "self-publish" and got this:

FUNNY YOU SHOULD ASK: HOW TO MARKET A BOOK 135

		Competitors			Earnings		Searches/Month		
⁞	214	>1,200	$12	$183					
⁞	170	91	$11	$271					
⁞	183	>1,200	$14	$121					
⁞	185	>1,200	$12	$778					
·	168	>1,200	$11	$92					
⁞	126	>1,200	$9	$2,831					
⁞	213	>1,200	$13	$388					
⁞	202	>1,200	$13	$237					
⁞	212	>1,200	$13	$148					
⁞	203	>1,200	$13	$128					
	201	221	$12	$12					
⁞	159	>1,200	$11	$296					

As usual, I have blurred out the actual keywords generated by this software out of respect for the developers of Publisher Rocket, but I just wanted to show you how many keywords and key phrases were generated just by starting with the phrase "self publish."

This is your place to quickly build a detailed keyword list for your book, plus it shows you which words and phrases are overly competitive, how much search traffic those words and phrases get, and how much the top-ranked books for those keywords are earning. This information is all great to know for your current book, and might even give you some ideas for other books you can write!

And that's it! File this keyword list in your "Marketing Research" folder, and be sure to go over and update the description and keyword boxes of your book if you haven't done so already. Even if your book has been out for years, there is never a bad time to give Amazon more information!

YOUR PRE-LAUNCH COUNTDOWN

OK, your network is in order and you've done all of your research to get your book found by Amazon's algorithm. Before you hit "publish" on your book, there are some things you'll need to do to make sure your launch month is as successful as possible. In a perfect world, you'll be reaching out to a large number (like, thousands) of advanced reviewers and sending them your book so they are ready to leave reviews during your launch month.

While you're waiting for them, you can go over your network with a fine-tooth comb to make sure it is solid and ready to grow, then schedule some paid promotional emails to go out during your launch month. Start these tasks 1-2 months before you publish to ensure you make the best use of the Amazon "honeymoon period."

13
THE SAFETY CHECKLISTS

You know how pilots have to do that final safety check before they fly a plane? And how you totally want them to do that, because if one tiny thing is wrong, it could mean the difference between life and death?

This is like that, but for your writing career. You'll want to perform this safety check any time you are about to start marketing a book, because you want the plane (your career) to take off and fly, and to stay in the sky.

We'll do this first for your book (since we just finished doing all that research), then we'll do it for your author platform. Also, yes, I am aware that I have already said all of this, so this chapter is probably redundant, but it's been a long haul and I want to give you a quick refresher before you run out into the world with your book in hand. I want you to succeed!

. . .

Let's start by pulling out your competitive analysis from Chapter 10. Now's when we're going to compare your book to its top 5-10 competitors.

We'll start in the most obvious place of all and judge your book by its cover.

1. Does your cover look like it belongs in the same category and subgenre as the 5-10 top-selling books? Is it eye-catching? Does it at least follow the design or color trends of the bestselling books? Do you think your book cover design is market-competitive? If not, would you consider having a different cover created? Your book's cover (and even more importantly, your book cover's thumbnail, which is what Amazon displays in its search results) is what sells the book to your potential readers. Without a strong, genre-competitive cover, you can throw thousands of marketing dollars at the book with little to no results. Would your marketing budget actually be better spent on getting a stronger cover? Give it some thought.

One way to tell if the problem is your cover is to start one or more paid ads through Amazon (which I cover in Chapter 20). If you get a bunch of impressions but no clicks (and no sales), people are not responding to your cover and you should definitely test a new one.

By the way, if you paid $2,000 for your cover and are thinking you would never even consider testing a different version, please just be willing to entertain the possibility that this might be the problem. You can get a new cover made for about $100 on Fiverr and can swap it out at any time if you published your book yourself.

You put a lot of time and effort into that book. Don't let stubbornness or pride over your cover hold you back!

2. Price. Is your book competitively priced in comparison to the top 5-10 books in that category or genre? If everyone else is charging $3.99 for their Kindle edition but you're charging $9.99 because you got some bad advice or didn't know any better when you published, please try changing the price to be more competitive. Before you argue that you don't want to accept less royalties, let me remind you that any percentage of zero sales is still zero.

3. Keywords. Did you put keywords in the seven backend keyword slots when you published your book? If not, there is a good chance Amazon is not showing your book to people because it doesn't know what the book is about. Now would be a great time to get out the keyword research from the last chapter and fill in those keyword slots.

4. Description. You (hopefully) read through all of your competitors' descriptions during the competitive analysis. Is your book's description comparable? Does it excite and motivate readers to want to know more about your story? If your book is nonfiction, does the "hook" of your book clearly indicate the problem that the book is solving? One way to test out whether your book description is decent is to run some paid advertising on it. If you get clicks but no sales, something is not grabbing people, and it might be the description.

5. The Book Itself. Maybe this goes without saying, and I certainly don't want to belabor this point or offend anyone, but I want to be

sure I cover all the bases in this guide. I'm not trying to tell you what to write, how to write, or even how to pick the genre in which you want to write. Write whatever you want—or if you're a publisher, publish whatever you want! *Just make sure anything you put out there is of the highest quality it can possibly be.* Assuming any book you have out there is the start of your potential audience members' (hopefully lifelong) interaction with you, your hope is that they like you enough to become your fan and buy your next book.

That is less likely to happen if the first thing they encounter is filled with typos and formatting errors, or if the cover is not up to par.

If your current book is with a traditional publisher, they are more than likely going to provide you with a team of people that will help you make the book the best it can be, so you are almost certain to end up with a product that you'll be proud of and will be confident to promote. If that is the case for you, feel free to skip this chapter, because I'm sure someone has already had this talk with you. Use the time you're saving to really get your author platform under control, and to start building that email list. Your publisher will probably be absolutely thrilled when you tell them you want to include a link inside the book to grow your email list, and that you have done all of your book's metadata research. In fact, they might even hire you as a consultant (it happened to me!).

If you're going to self-publish (or you already did), or if your book is with a smaller publisher where you might be participating in the process a little more, there are a few areas where you're going to need to be a little more diligent in order to ensure that your book is the best it can be, because trust me, you do not want to spend all that time getting your book ranked in Amazon only to make the horrifying discovery that it is filled with typos (something you will find out about when it starts getting slammed by reviewers and amasses multiple one-star reviews). These things are bad and might scar you for your author life, so just make sure your book is ready for prime time before you start this book marketing journey.

OK, so your book is good? You went through this list and checked off every single thing?

Great. Let's just go over your author platform once more before you go out into the book marketing wild. Here are the elements I would like you to have in place before you launch your book:

1. **The Right Attitude.** You've gotten your head around the fact that you do need to market your book and are hopefully going to make book marketing a part of your everyday life. Fantastic!

2. **An Organizational System That Works for You.** This means you have a centralized and organized place for all of your logins, links, book covers, photos, bios, finalized manuscripts, and anything else anyone could possibly ask for when they're trying to help you promote your book. You should be able to easily find anything book- or author-related quickly and easily. Once your book takes off, you're going to be super busy, and you don't want opportunities to fall through the cracks because you couldn't find your most recent book cover or the link to your book.

. . .

3. **An Email List + Lead Magnet + Link.** This means you have an account with an email marketing service, a proper landing page with an incentivized offer plus an automated delivery email, and a link to this page within all of your books. Before you launch your book, enter your own email into this signup box one last time and make sure the "Welcome" autoresponder email successfully arrives and that you can download it. These are all parts of your "list," which you might now recognize as the thing I think is the most important thing in your author life.

4. **A Fantastic Onboarding Sequence.** This series of emails will get new people familiar with you and your work, get them used to hearing from you, and offer them other things you have for sale. You can also use these emails to request reviews and to get new people into your launch team.

5. **A Fully Functional Author Website.** This is not something that you absolutely need in order to launch, but I would really like you to have it since your book is going to get you some attention (ideally), and I would like people to be able to go to your website, learn more about you, and sign up for your email list. When your book blows up, you want to be easy to find for interviews! I'm going to assume that your website is already set up, so before you launch, just go over there and make sure everything looks and functions the way you want it to. Test the email signup to make sure it works. Test the "Contact Us" form to make sure emails that get sent through it actually arrive in your inbox. Click every single link on your website to make sure they all work, and that they go where you want them to go. What you don't want is for a famous New York City publisher to be trying to email you to offer you a million bucks for your next book, only to find that the "Contact Us" link on your website is broken. DO NOT LET THIS HAPPEN TO YOU You

will also want to make sure your press kit is in order if media appearances are something you're pursuing.

6. **Social Media With No "Leaks."** Go to each and every one of your social media platforms and make sure there is a link in your profile with either a LinkTree URL that contains all of your pertinent links, or that takes you back to your author website. Check your Twitter, LinkedIn, Facebook Author Page, Pinterest, and whatever other social media profiles you have established over the years (or in Chapter 6). If you have a YouTube channel, make sure your author website and book links are in the description of every single video on that channel. I am not joking! I am willing to bet that you will find one or more places where you either don't have a link at all, or you have a link that doesn't work or is from an old website you were trying a long time ago (like for a specific book or an idea you had). This is the number-one place where I see authors losing potential readers, and that's a crying shame, because it's so easy to fix. Also, for any social media platform that does not give you the opportunity to include an actual link, include a reference to something like your Twitter that does have the link. What you want is to make it as simple as humanly possible for people to learn more about you and to buy your stuff. While you're on each social media platform, go ahead and make sure all of your information is current, remove anything that is really dated (or controversial), and post something new to wake up the algorithm of that platform. You don't want your first post back in three years of not being on Twitter to be a "Hey, I have a new book! Buy my new book!" post, because people hate that kind of thing and social media platforms aren't super enthusiastic about showing stuff like that. What I'm saying is, please go to each platform where you have a presence and at least pretend to be an active user in the week or two before your book launches.

· · ·

7. Presence on the Book Sites. You are going to be super bummed out if most of the reviewers you approach are on Goodreads and you never set up your profile over there. Just saying.

8. Proper Measurement. By that I mean, how will you know if and when your marketing efforts succeed? Now is the time to decide what metrics are important to you and put measurement in place to track those. For example, are you measuring mailing list signups? If that's important to you, definitely have your email service provider email you when you get a new signup. Do you even know how many books you're selling every day or how many page reads you're getting through Kindle Unlimited? Sign up for KDChamp (https://kdpchamp.com) , and they will send you an email when you make a sale (or when someone reads your book through KENP). They can even let you know when your book gets ratings or reviews!

All done? Great! Let's talk about sending your book out to thousands of potential reviewers.

14
REVIEWS, PART I: THE ARC STORY

Reviews! You know you need them for your book to succeed. But, how many do you need, where do you get them, and when do you start working on them? To answer that question, I am going to jump right in and start talking about a concept that might be brand-new to you: the Advanced Reader Copy, or ARC (also called an eARC because ARCS are mostly electronic these days). ARC refers to your finalized manuscript (or as finalized as it's ever going to be, to the point where you could publish it that day), and it's the version of your book that you'll send out to reviewers for the purpose of getting things like early/editorial reviews to put in your Amazon listing and in your press materials, pull quotes you can use on your book cover, and regular reviews on places like Amazon, GoodReads, and other outlets.

If you're wondering why you would go to all this trouble, here's why: You send out ARCs before you publish your book to get a lot of reviews (and sometimes publicity in the form of mentions on social media) when the book comes out, and you do this because you need reviews and publicity to sell books (especially within Amazon, where reviews are the equivalent of search engine backlinks).

To determine how far you need to venture down into this ARC rabbit hole, I will direct you back to your competitive analysis. The sixty-four thousand-dollar question here is, what is the average number of reviews of the other books appearing for your chosen keyphrase? **If that number is something like 500, that's how many reviews you're going to need,** and I'm sorry for both of us if your book is already out and this is the first you're hearing of this. For your book to have a chance at "sticking" on page one for that search phrase once its honeymoon period has passed, it needs to have at least as many reviews as the other books appearing for that phrase, if not more. Amazon's not going to expect you to get all of those reviews in your book's first month, but there does have to be some indication that your book is going in that direction, and a large ARC team is how you make that happen.

To help further explain this concept and why it's important, here's an example, pulled from our fascinating paranormal-shifter romance analysis in Chapter 10. I have blocked out the covers out of respect for the authors who didn't achieve the results they were probably wanting, because I truly do not mean to disparage anyone's efforts. I'm just here to look at results and draw speculative conclusions about what went right or wrong based on those results, and you don't really need to know the author names or book titles for that.

FUNNY YOU SHOULD ASK: HOW TO MARKET A BOOK 149

From that first analysis, you might recall that I determined (with my calculator!) the average review count for that subgenre to be 1,150, so let's see how these competitors are doing compared to that.

I did this competitive analysis on May 13, 2022. Book #1 had just come out the week before, and amassed about 63 reviews in its first week. When I repeated the analysis on June 22nd, book one was no longer on page one for that search phrase. Upon further investigation, I discovered that book one had only gotten 329 reviews in its first six weeks of life, which would explain its disappearance. This is pure speculation on my part, but it does seem like Amazon's algorithm gave this book's slot away to a new release when it didn't get a competitive amount of reviews. Just my opinion!

Don't get me wrong—329 reviews is A LOT, and I am not trying to disparage that person's effort (which is why I blocked out the cover and the author's name). However, if this author wants this book to be found for paranormal-shifter romance, they will need to get an additional 700 reviews. There is every chance this author will eventually get the required number of reviews to get this book back onto page one, provided they get enough people onto their regular email list and ask them for reviews in their onboarding sequence (and in the book itself). It's going to take awhile, but this is a doable goal, and since this author has everything set up properly and has 34 books on their backlist, they will get there.

Book two is not faring as well, and let's talk about why. When I did the initial analysis, this book had four reviews, some of which were two stars (for grammar and typos). That's already not great. This author needed to employ a good editor and proofreader before they put their book out, because it's tough to get great reviews on an inferior product. Upon further analysis, it became clear that this author is apparently not actively doing anything to get reviews, so those bad reviews were going to really impact the overall average going forward. When I followed up in July, this book only had 14 reviews and had completely disappeared from the search results for the phrase paranormal-shifter romance, presumably because it failed Amazon's "honeymoon period" test.

When I looked a little more closely into this author's Author Central page (which, by the way, was not filled out properly and had zero information about their website, how to find them on social, or how to get on their email list), I found that almost all of their books had this issue with low review numbers. This author has several problems that are impacting their overall sales: poor quality product, improperly set up author platform, and the apparent lack of an ARC review team. These three factors alone are especially deadly when you consider they are trying to swim in the paranormal-shifter romance pond and compete against authors like the one we're about to talk about.

Book three, "Chase Me," which is the clear winner of this contest, came out in February of 2018 and has stuck to page one of the paranormal-shifter romance results like glue. It had 1320 reviews when I did the analysis in May of 2022 and 1445 reviews when I went back to check it in July. From these excellent results, I can surmise that this person had a strong ARC team in place when they launched, or that they have an extremely large email list and subscriber base. This author has over 50 books on their backlist, a fantastic website with a clear path to email signup, and profiles on all the social media platforms that point people right back to that website and email list. It's almost as if that author did every single thing I have outlined in this book, and that those things worked! IMAGINE THAT!

Ideally I've now convinced you that putting in the work with ARCs pays off in the long run, because I am about to hit you with another big reality check. Since about 25%-40% of the ARCs you send out are going to result in actual reviews, you will need to look at your competitive analysis, calculate how many reviews you would need for your book to be competitive, and try to find two-to-three times that many ARC readers. In the case of paranormal-shifter romance, that would mean sending out about 3,000 ARCs and following up until you got to the goal of 1,150 reviews.

Before you panic and throw this book across the room, please consider that ARC strategy is one of those subjects where everyone has a different opinion about when and how to send your ARCs, which services to use, when to follow up, and so on. I'm not here to weigh in on any of that, because what works for a romance author might not work for their non-fiction author friend, and so on. Your ARC strategy is going to depend on how much time (and patience) you have and how many reviews you need, so I'm going to give you all of the overview information about the ARC world and let you take it from there. Some authors totally skip this step, and that's fine for you to do if you are in a less competitive genre/subcategory and don't need that many reviews. My goal here is to give you the 30,000-foot view of the concept of ARCs and to point you in the direction of ARC-related resources and services so you can plan your strategy accordingly.

Okay. Let's just take a second and do a TL;DR of the last couple of pages, so that we're all caught up: ARCs are advanced review (or advanced reader) copies. You send those out prior to the book's release, for free and for the purpose of obtaining honest reviews. You then follow up to make sure people read the book and remind them to post their reviews. The number of ARCs to send out is based on the average review count of the books in the competitive analysis you did back in Chapter 10, so take this number, multiply it by two or three, and send out that many ARCs. **You will need to create your own ARC strategy based on your genre and the number of reviews you need.** Getting a ton of ARC reviews when you launch basically comes down to finding enough people, getting them to agree to read and review your book, and following up with them.

This is when it would be amazing to have your ARC team already assembled (that would be your segmented email list of superfans who will read your work and leave you reviews). You build this team by inviting people from your regular email list to join, and this can be done in the fifth email of your onboarding sequence. If people make it that far, there's a good chance they like hearing from you and would like to become one of your reviewers. You can also advertise your need for ARC readers directly on your author website and your social media, because the best place to find reviewers is from your own pool of existing readers. In this case, you would just manage the delivery of the ARC and the follow-up yourself. You can use BookFunnel (which we referenced during the set-up for your lead magnet) to seamlessly deliver your ARCs. BookFunnel also has newsletter swaps and author promos to help you build up your list of readers.

See how far we've come on our book marketing journey? At the beginning of this book, you wouldn't have been able to decipher one word of that last paragraph. I'm so proud. I'm assuming you only just started your email list and haven't segmented it down yet, which is fine (as long as you have your main email list signup in place). Your ARC team can grow over time.

Let's just address what has become the elephant in the room, which is: where are you supposed to find ARC readers if you don't already have a list? I actually have three answers to that question, and here they are:

1. Look for People on Social Media Who Already Read that Genre

. . .

This is when you're going to be so happy you set up your social media properly back in Chapter 6 and have now updated it with your book cover, because the next best way to find ARC reviewers is to search for them on social media and pitch them your book. There are many ways to search, but here are two of my favorites:

First, grab your list of competitive authors from Chapter 10. Using your preferred method of social media (let's use Instagram for this example), visit the social media profiles of those authors and start following people who follow them. You already know that these people are fans of the thing you write, so you'll want to go through them one by one and look for people who like those authors and also do book reviews. In this method of ARC reader acquisition, you actually want a reviewer with a smaller social media following, because that person is more than likely trying to become a professional reviewer and will therefore do a great job on your review to prove him or herself (provided they like your book, which they will because you spent the time making sure that book and its cover are nothing short of award-winningly amazing).

Is this method time-consuming and tedious? Yes it is! This is the kind of thing you'll need to start months before your book launches, and keep building it up over time. The more competitive your genre/subcategory, the more reviews you'll need, so the more time you'll need to put in to grow this team of enthusiastic supporters.

Does it work? Yes, it does! In fact, this is the exact method I used to push my debut novel, "Hollywood Car Wash," up and over the top, eventually selling so many copies that Simon & Schuster bought and re-released it. I basically spent a year using MySpace to connect with 12,000 people who had read and enjoyed "The Devil Wears Prada" or "The Nanny Diaries" and telling them about my book, and it worked!

Yes, I said MySpace. Look, it was 2006. MySpace was all we had. You have it so much better now because there are so many more social media outlets and ways to build up people on them.

While you're on social media finding potential fans and building your audience, keep your eye out for the other type of person you'll need to add to your ARC team: book reviewers. I'm listing them second because a lot of them are not going to give you the time of day if you're not already a well-known author with a big following and already established book sales.

2. Look for Book Reviewers Who Review What You Write

For this method, you'll search by the hashtag for your genre, like #paranormalromance, like this:

There you go! 410,207 posts with the hashtag "paranormal romance." You will just need to go through these one by one, looking for readers and reviewers who might want to cover your book. Be sure that your profile is fully filled out and that you have your ARC ready to go. This is really a numbers game, because you'll need to keep reaching out to people and pitching them until you get to that 2X-to-3X number of ARC copies sent out. You can also go to https://booksirens.com/book-reviewer-directory to look for book reviewers (in your genre, of course). For more information on what to actually say to people, I have compiled some more info at https://bookpromotion.com/ARC

. . .

Even if you don't have time to connect with potential fans on social media prior to the launch of this book, that's fine! Definitely start doing this at some point though, because you can never have too many readers or members of your ARC team!

We have now covered the efforts that will cost you more time than money, so let's move on to paid services, because sometimes you just have to throw money at the problem. I get it!

3. Use ARC Services

ARC services can help you get readers and manage the delivery and follow-up of your ARC, so there are definite advantages to going this route. Also, if you strike up good relationships with ARC readers on one or more of these services, there is a chance they might join your personal ARC team going forward.

Here are the major services, listed in alphabetical order. Of course, I will throw out the (slightly major) caveat that not all of these services are going to cater to all genres and categories, so please do research to make sure the service you choose actually has enough ARC readers that read and review your genre. Choosing an ARC service is not unlike when you settled on your favorite social media platform—you'll need to take a look at each one to see if your "people" are on there and if the service is going to do what you need. Whatever you do, do NOT sign up for an ARC service that doesn't segment by genre, because the last thing you need is cross-genre reviews, which are notoriously poor. I did not know this when I first published, and I learned the hard way when a person one-starred my debut novel because he (and he wrote this in the review) "prefers books on opera."

Book Sirens

BookSirens has 20,000 readers and reviewers in its database and boasts an impressive 75% review rate. The pricing for their "promote" service is a little weird ($10 to put an ARC on the site, then $2 per "claim" when people sign up to read and review it), so if you need a bunch of reviews, I would just go ahead and get the Author plan for $100/year. https://booksirens.com/pricing

BookSprout

BookSprout has 65,000 readers who might want to review your book, so that's already a good start. They also rank and rate their reviewers, so you can check people out before handing your book over to them. BookSprout used to be free, but in March of 2022 they redesigned and relaunched, and now all of their options are paid. You can find those at https://booksprout.com/pricing. If you need a bunch of reviews, I would recommend getting the "Bestseller" plan ($29/month) for at least a few months prior to your launch. BookSprout is known to yield the best results for romance authors, so keep that in mind.

NetGalley

NetGalley is the ARC review service the big publishers use, and they have by far the most readers in their database (upwards of 550,000). Their pricing used to be prohibitive for indie authors and publishers, but they have recently made some changes and have just recently put out some service offerings that are tailored to us. It's still the most expensive, but they have the biggest reach and will usually get you the most reviews, so they can be a good option for you if you have the budget. NetGalley has never been super transparent about their pricing, but Kindlepreneur did a fantastic breakdown of the different offering levels (and how to get discounts on each), which I have linked to right here: https://bookpromotion.com/netgalley

I know I've hit you with a lot of information in this chapter, and your mind is probably reeling (either with possibilities or general overwhelm). Hang in there! I have a whole other chapter on getting reviews after your book has launched, so go ahead and put everything in place to start growing your ARC team for future releases.

Once you've gotten ARCs to everyone on your team, it's time to start planning your launch and setting up promotional emails that will happen during that month. Take a breather, because we're about to go into a whole other mammoth topic!

15
BOOK PROMOTION SITES

Another way to get your book out there is to put it on one or more paid promotional sites that have big email lists of readers. There are tons of these promo sites out there, and you can schedule promotional emails for right after your book launches. It's good to schedule them while you're waiting for your ARC reviewers to read your book and get back to you.

Yep, it's another one of those "all-day sucker" topics. Let's break it down and talk a little more about how this all works, then you can go as far down the "paid promotion" rabbit hole as your time and money (and patience) allow. Maybe this will be the book marketing method that you love and use for every launch going forward!

What's a promo site?

A promo site is basically a person or company with a big (hopefully segmented by genre) email list of people that want free or discounted books. The "800-pound gorilla" of the book promo space is BookBub so I'll tell you about them first, but there are many (many!) others that we'll talk about here. It is a good idea to set a bunch of these up to happen in a row during your launch month, which is called "promo stacking" even though the promos usually happen consecutively rather than all on the same day. As with all of the other promotional tools I have mentioned, the goal with promotional emails is to get traffic and sales activity going to your book throughout your launch month so Amazon knows your book is worth continuing to show for your focus keywords. If your book is already out there and you're trying to revive it, you can also use promo stacking as a way to breathe some life (and hopefully new sales) back and to get Amazon to start noticing it for your focus keywords (because you've updated your metadata, right?!)

—When/why do you do promos?

Generally speaking, I'm fine with authors doing promos anytime, but if you have a limited budget, the best time to do them is within 30 days of your book's launch, because that's when you're going to see the largest "bang for your buck" with Amazon. You would use paid promos to get more visibility for your book, get reviews, and to try to trigger Amazon's algorithm to show it for your chosen keywords.

. . .

—What are the different promo sites? Which one is the best?

There are a bunch of them, so I will describe the major ones I think you should know about and consider.

First up: let's talk about BookBub, which we set up as one of the book sites in your author platform in Chapter 7. I also recommended that you sign up for their free email list, so you've hopefully been receiving their emails and are familiar with them by now. BookBub is where we all have to start, and you can't really write a book on book marketing without mentioning them so I'm doing that.

Here's the thing with BookBub, and I hope if anyone from there is reading this they have a sense of humor: BookBub is kind of the worst. It's super hard to even get offered a deal with them (like, they only take 10-20% of books that get submitted), and if you can even manage to convince them to pick your book, their promotions are a small fortune. If you think I am exaggerating, get your smelling salts ready and head over to their price list: https://www.bookbub.com/partners/pricing

I KNOW! It's so expensive!. The problem is, they have 10 million readers, so they can make or break your career. While indie publishers would love to just shun BookBub before they reject us, we can't, because that much exposure (combined with a solid author platform and properly optimized book, of course!) can put you on the map. I guess what I'm saying is, if you try to ignore them, it only hurts you.

. . .

If you looked at that pricing sheet and BookBub is not something you can even consider right now, that is totally fine. There's nothing saying you HAVE to submit your book for a deal, and you can always submit it later once you have some book income to reinvest. I did just want you to know about it first so you could submit your book if that's the place you're in right now. To submit a book, you'll need to have already set up your BookBub partners account (which is why we did that back in Chapter 7). If your book is a new release, you can submit it to the "New Releases for Less" promo at https://partners.bookbub.com/new_release_promotions/.

If your book didn't just come out so it's not eligible for a new release deal, you can still submit it on your regular dashboard, and you'll want to regularly submit books for consideration if you have the budget and the backlist. There's no harm in trying to get in if you can afford it! Here are the submission requirements for books in general: https://www.bookbub.com/partners/requirements

If the last couple of paragraphs discouraged you, I apologize! I just wanted to level-set when it comes to BookBub.

Promoting Your Book When/ If It Is Free:

These are the ones you'll schedule to coincide with your KDP Select free days if you're doing those. This is something I would only recommend doing during the launch of a brand-new book, because you are obviously not going to make back the cost of the promo if you're giving your book away for free. Oh, also– "free promo" in this context means that *your book* is free, not that the promo is free.

FreeBooksy.com — FreeBooksy usually has the longest lead time, so I would recommend scheduling your free days around what they have available, then booking the other sites from there. The cost of a FreeBooksy promo ranges from $30 - $120, depending on your genre. FreeBooksy is the leader (after BookBub, of course) in the paid promotion space, with thousands of targeted readers on multiple email lists.

Once you've scheduled your FreeBooksy promo, work your way down this list depending on how much budget you have left You'll need all of these promos to go out over the five-day period of your KDP Select days, so schedule them carefully and BE ABSOLUTELY SURE to make a note in your calendar to start your free days on KDP the night before the first promo! This is super important!

Here are the other sites I recommend for promoting your free book days.

– ENT (EReader News Today): $40 - $50

–BookDoggy: $18

–Fussy Librarian: $10 - $30

. . .

You can do one or more of these as your budget allows, but you will need to be sure to schedule all of them for the time period when your book is free. KDP Select allows for five free days– you can do these in a row if that's how your promos end up lining up, or you can spread them over multiple days. Totally up to you (and your excellent time management skills!). I do all of my days in a row because I am more of a "set it and forget it" type of person.

In case you're curious (or if you're wanting to save some money on this step), yes, there are sites where you can promote your free book for free. More of them pop up every single day, actually! The issues there are: how much time do you have to submit your book to every single service, and are the services even reputable? If you want to do more research, I have an ongoing list of links to book promotion services galore over at https://bookpromotion.com/promos

The purpose of the "giving your book away for free" strategy is threefold: you use it to get reviews, to train Amazon's algorithm to show your book for your keywords, and to get people to sign up for your email list through the reader magnet link in your book. However, is fine if you don't want to use a "free book" strategy! You have to decide what is right for you based on your goals and budget. I totally understand that some authors do not want to give their books away under any circumstances.

Discounted Book Promotions

The other way to do paid promos is to pay for placement on "discounted" book lists, meaning you set your book's price at something like 99 cents (or $1 or $2 off of your regular price. If you're done with the free promo (or you skipped it, no shade, free is not for everyone), you then schedule the discounted promo days. For a typical launch, I will usually do my free promo days the first week after the book goes live, then drop the price to 99 cents during the second week and do some paid promos on that.

Here are the discounted book promo sites I use the most:

–BargainBooksy : $20 - $240

–BookDoggy ($20)

–**ENT** ($45-$120)

– **Fussy Librarian** ($10-$22)

Many of the sites that will promote a free book for free will also promote discounted books, and you can find a running list of those over at https://bookpromotion.com/promos

The whole concept of promotional emails is a little dense, so I hope we've made some headway in your understanding here and given you a place to start. Remember, the real purpose of promotional emails is to get your book some reviews, to raise the visibility of your books, and to "train" Amazon's algorithm to show your book for keywords, so don't be too upset if you don't make back the full amount you paid for the promos. Sometimes book marketing is a long game!

PART 3: YOUR LAUNCH

You made it! Yay!

If you were pre-launch when you picked up this book, hopefully you've now made all of your updates and hit "Publish" on your book, you've passed the Amazon review period, and all of your book's editions (Kindle, paperback, and hardcover) have gone live.

You are now in the race of your life, against the ticking clock that is the Amazon "honeymoon period," where the all-knowing Amazon algorithm is going to show your book to its millions (billions?) of customers when they search your main keywords. This is that "throw everything at it" moment where you'll want to really do every single thing you can think of to get sales over to this book.

If you didn't catch the honeymoon period this time around, that's also ok! You can still follow along and do all of the things I mention here, then put paid advertising on your book to artificially replicate the organic traffic of the honeymoon period.

16

GET REVIEWS

Here we are, back on the subject of reviews. In Chapter 14, we talked about how to determine how many you need, how to start building up a team of people who will do them for you, and where to look for people to review your book.

Hopefully you've gotten ARCs of your book out to reviewers and your ARC team weeks and weeks in advance of your launch (on social media or sites like BookSprout and BookSirens,) and you are now following up like crazy and racking up the early reviews. It would be SO GREAT if that were all in place already and your reviews were rolling in, and the next time through, that will be the case since you will have built all of this into the publishing and marketing process from the beginning. The good news is, if you write a great book and put the initial effort into optimizing it properly and getting its momentum going with its initial reviews from your ARC team, eventually the snowball effect will kick in and strangers will start reviewing it without being asked. You have to get to that tipping point though!

I know we're all coming to this book marketing party from very different starting points, so I did just want to give you some ways to get reviews if your book is already out and/or your ARC team is still growing. You can use just one of these, combine the ones that appeal to you, or use them all until your book gets to the desired number of reviews to get it selling organically through Amazon (since that is the ultimate goal).

Here are a bunch of ways to get reviews going to your book.

1. Put a review request inside the book itself. OK, your book is fantastic, but now you've got to actually ask people to review it. The place to do that is inside the book itself. You're offering people a free incentive or reader magnet at the front of your book (to get them to sign up for your email list), so why not ask them for a review while they're reading (and hopefully enjoying) it?

I have always just put review requests at the back of the book because I felt like people needed to read the whole book before they could review it. However, I recently spotted a review request in the actual body content/copy of a book I was reading, so I decided to investigate to see if this strategy was effectively converting reviews. To my absolute shock, this method appears to work better than anything I have ever seen or tried, and I am now in the process of integrating it into my backlist.

. . .

Instead of appearing in the back matter, the review request appears at the 1/3 and 2/3 marks in the book. Initially, I was skeptical of how effective this would be because I personally thought it distracted from the content, but when I went to look at how many reviews this book had, I quickly had to eat my words.

Over 2300 reviews in 2 1/2 years, you guys!

If you're not quite at this level yet, just stick a review request in the back matter of the book and call it good. Amazon will also hit people up for a review (or rating) if the reader gets all the way to the end of the Kindle edition, but you can't guarantee how many people are actually going to get there, so you should definitely include it.

2. Ask friends and family. This is where everyone always starts, and I don't object to it because our friends and family are usually our first customers, but tread carefully here. Not only do you not want to irritate your loved ones with repeated review requests, but Amazon is cracking down on reviews that come from people who are obviously and blatantly related to you. What I'm saying is, lower your expectations of any review actually sticking where the person has your same last name. And if the reviewer says "The author is my best friend!", that is also not ideal. But you're not going to have to worry about all of this, because eventually your book marketing game is going to be so strong that you'll never have to hit up your friends and family again. Onward!

3. Ask in Facebook groups. Depending on your genre, you might be a member of one or more Facebook groups that pertain to that

thing. Surely some of the people in those groups would like a free copy of your book in exchange for an honest review! This works much better if you can work with the admin of the group in question to post a "free review copy in exchange for honest reviews" type post. Use BookFunnel to deliver the review copy or direct them over to a new campaign at BookSprout or whatever ARC service you ended up using in Chapter 14.

4. Ask in subreddits. Same concept, but pertaining to subreddits you might be a member of (say, for your subject matter).

5. Use an ARC service to run a review campaign for an already-launched book. In chapter 15, I covered all the ways to run a conventional ARC campaign, but you can also go back through that list and run those campaigns for existing books.

6. Build a review request into your email onboarding sequence. You probably need things to put in your fourth or fifth email anyway, so why not include a link for the person to review your book if they're so inclined? In my experience, the less you have to make people work for this the more likely they are to actually do it, so provide them with a direct link to the actual place to leave the review.

In link form that looks like this: https://www.amazon.com/review/create-review/?ie=UTF8&channel=glance-detail&asin=XXXXXXX

Replace "XXXXXX" with your ASIN number.

. . .

To find this on Amazon (for copy and pasting purposes), you'll go to your book's listing, then scroll down until you see this on the left:

Review this product

Share your thoughts with other customers

Write a customer review

Click "Write a customer review," then copy the url of that link and stick it in your "Administrative/Book Details" file so you won't have to go searching for it the next time you need it. This is what you'll send out, because again, people tend to be lazy, so you need to do everything you can do to get them at close as you can to the moment they write that review (short of taking their hands and putting them on the keyboard, a thing we all wish we could do!).

7. Use Pubby. Another paid service (not paid reviews! There is a difference—don't pay for reviews!), Pubby is my current favorite place to get reviews. This is a paid platform where authors can upload their books, review others' books, and get reviews for their books. It is totally within Amazon's terms of service because it is actually impossible for two authors to review each other's work. Individual authors can review up to 10 books per week, earning "snaps" (points) for each book reviewed. https://bookpromotion.com/pubby to get started.

. . .

Here's how it works: you sign up (there is no free level), list your book, put however many specifications you want on your book (like "required/verified purchase" or "OK to read for free using Kindle Unlimited," then sign up to review other people's books. Note: Pubby appears to only work for established U.S. Amazon accounts.

8. Use KDP select to offer your book for free, then run a paid promotion. We are going all the way into this in the very next chapter, but I wanted to just introduce the concept here so it's on your radar. This is a very effective technique for getting reviews just because of the sheer number of downloads you get when you put your book for free, then advertise it to thousands of people.

Try all of these methods until you get to your desired number of reviews!

17
PAID ADVERTISING OVERVIEW

If you want to pay to get your book out there faster, Amazon Advertising is, in my opinion, the best bang for your buck. Unlike other types of paid advertising, Amazon Ads get you access to millions and millions of actual buyers who have their credit cards out and are ready to buy. Amazon ads are the best way to ease yourself into paying for ads for your book, because they are relatively easy to set up, they exist in the same world where you published and you can see if they result in sales. My goal for this chapter is to help you get through the initial setup of your first Amazon Ads. If you're looking for information on other types of paid advertising (like Facebook and BookBub), I have put information about those over at https://bookpromotion.com/ads. I would love to tell you more about those types of advertising, but I make it a policy to only talk about things that I have actually tried out on my own books. Since I haven't used anything but Amazon Ads, I found you some authoritative sources for the other two types.

. . .

However, before we dive into Amazon Ads, let's just pump the brakes for a moment and determine whether your book is even ready for ads. So we're very clear on this, I do not think you should spend one penny on ads for your books if you don't have everything set up properly and you've already made some organic sales. Paid advertising is for scaling a system that is already working! It is not a cure-all for poor setup! If you don't have some properly optimized metadata, a reader magnet link inside your book to get people onto your email list, and a few reviews, do not pass go! You are not ready for paid advertising!

That was a lot of exclamation points, I know. I just really, really don't want you to waste money on ads, ok?

Some of you are going to ignore my advice and start running ads anyway, and that is fine. I accept that some authors want to throw money at the problem and start seeing book sales right away. HOWEVER, the link to the reader magnet signup is the one real deal-breaker for me. God forbid you hit upon a winning ad combination on the first try and your book ends up a bestseller. If that happens and you don't have a way for people to sign up for your email list, you will kick yourself (and I will kick you if you tell me about it!). You are literally PAYING for opportunities to acquire new customers, so don't waste that money by just settling for a one-time royalty! As I've said enough times to get on your nerves, every book is a chance to build your career by getting one more person on your email list where you can sell them more books in the future. Ultimately, I believe that the goal of paid advertising should be to build up your email list so you don't continue to need more paid advertising. Imagine that!

. . .

FUNNY YOU SHOULD ASK: HOW TO MARKET A BOOK

Assuming you have heeded my final warnings about that all-important email signup, let's get started with Amazon advertising. I have some strong-ish feelings about the way Amazon has designed its paid advertising interface, and the more I write about them, the more I seem like a conspiracy theorist, but here we are.

Oh! One more thing, before we get too far into this. You will NOT be able to run paid advertising on your book if it has swear words on the cover or if Amazon determines that your cover or subject matter is "too racy," meaning the cover or the content has adult themes. If you know your book is probably going to get rejected and you don't want to spend the time learning how to set up paid ads, that's fair! Skip this chapter and come back for this information later when you have a book this applies to.

So, paid advertising. If you haven't already, go over and start your Amazon advertising account at advertising.amazon.com, or go to one of the books in your library, click the three dots next to the book, and select "Promote and Advertise." That looks like this:

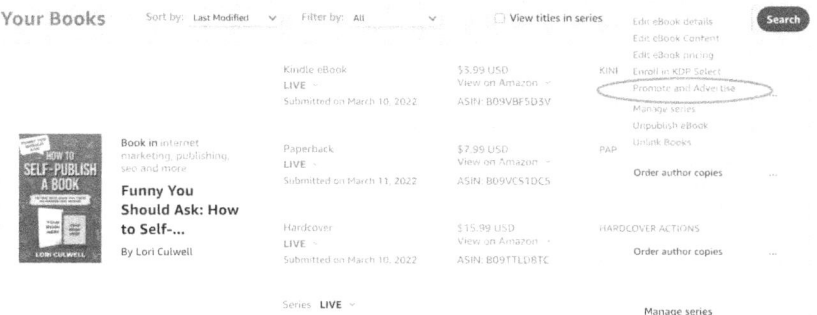

You will need to set up your advertising account and enter a payment method (credit or debit) because you are going to be paying for your ads in advance, even though Amazon is going to pay you 60 days after a sale (meaning if you sell a book today, you receive your royalties two months from now). Is that fair? Not really. But, Amazon runs the show, so we play by their rules.

As you can tell from the above example, I'm about to walk you through the setup for each one of these for my book "Funny You Should Ask: How to Self Publish a Book," because why not? What we need in this book marketing book is clearly more examples of marketing a book that is also about books. That's not confusingly meta.

First, choose a campaign type. You want "Sponsored Products," unless you have a series of books that you've built into a whole brand with its own Author Central page. I'm assuming this is your first time through the Amazon Ads interface and you don't have a whole branded series built up yet, so put a pin in that for the future and come back to it when you have a series.

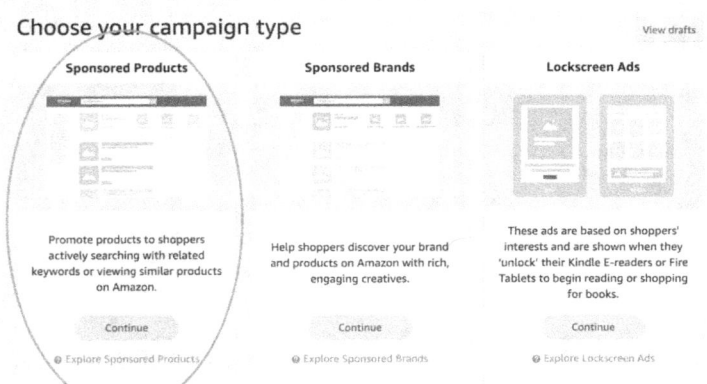

FUNNY YOU SHOULD ASK: HOW TO MARKET A BOOK 181

I will tell you the settings I use for these ads and give you my reasoning behind each choice. Of course, feel free to change things up based on your own experiences, goals, and budget. Do what you want! I'm just telling you what works for me.

First off, I always just do "standard ad." I have tried the kind with the fancy custom ad text, and I found that those ads didn't convert as well as standard ads (maybe because custom ad text makes it look more like an ad?). Also, custom ad text is a pain to write because you have to suddenly be an expert copywriter who can entice readers with a short and punchy headline. If that is you, try the custom text ad. If not, please join me in choosing "standard ad."

Ad Format   ⓘ Choosing your ad format

   Custom text ad
   Add custom text to your ad to give customers a glimpse of the book.
⦿ Standard ad
   Choose this option to advertise your products without custom text.

Find the book you want to advertise under Products (this will already be selected if you came to the ad interface by clicking "promote and advertise" next to the book), then scroll down to targeting. We're going with "Manual" targeting, and I'll tell you why.

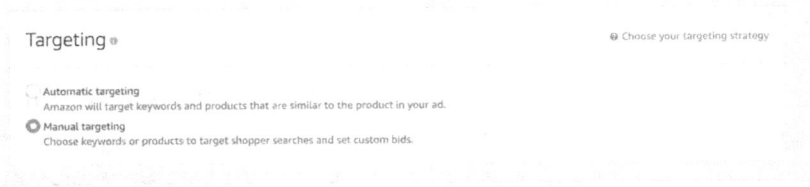

Here's where I start to sound paranoid, but go with me because I'm ranting about something that benefits you. I'm pretty sure Amazon has set this entire advertising interface up to monetize your lack of knowledge about how advertising works, and that all starts with auto-targeted ads, which are a terrible idea. Mostly I think these are Amazon's way of getting easy money from you based on your desire to get through this advertising interface as quickly as possible, and I resent that. They know full well that ads with manually-targeted keywords convert much better than their automated ads, but they push you toward auto ads because it's good money for them and you don't know any better.

Auto ads, in case you don't know (and why would you?) are ads where Amazon picks the keywords and products to advertise your book against automatically, based on what they know about your book. If they don't know what your book is about (because, for example, you didn't fill in your metadata properly and don't have a keyword-rich title, subtitle, or description), they are not going to tell you that. Instead, they are basically going to charge you to show your book when people search for random crap that has nothing to do with it (like, at all). If you rush through the setup of that ad because you didn't know any better, you're going to be super upset when you find that you've spent $25, made zero sales, and don't even have any good keywords to show for it.

. . .

My point is this: the only purpose of an Amazon auto ad is basically to get you to pay Amazon to find you some good keywords, products, and categories to populate your manual ad campaigns, and since you already did all that great research back in Chapter 12, you can skip the auto ad step (and expense) because you already have lists of keywords, categories, and comparable products ready to go. You've done a crap-ton of research, so you know what your book is about, and you told Amazon by optimizing your metadata properly. You don't need this "feeling around in the dark" step, so save your money and skip the auto ads.

The ad we're doing is a keyword ad, so pick "Manual Targeting>Keyword Targeting," which looks like this:

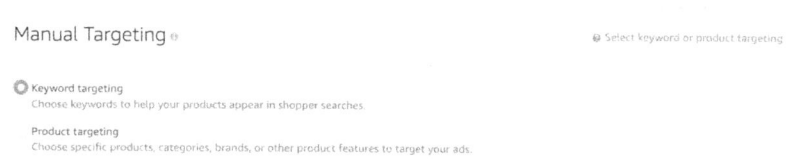

You would think that since you've chosen "manual," Amazon would know that you want to enter your own keywords, but they are going to try one more layer of automated "suggestions" on the very first screen of the keyword targeting interface. Once you see the words they are suggesting for my self-publishing book, you're going to laugh and realize why you should never let Amazon pick keywords for you (either in automated ads or right here). Because, my friends, this book's metadata is optimized to the hilt. I did a proper launch, and it is already ranking for 250+ publishing-related keywords. Yet, despite all this, here is the first screen of Amazon's "suggestions" for advertising keywords.

Keywords IS | IR	Match type	Sugg. bid Regular days	Add all
blogging	Broad	$0.54	Add
IS: 0	Phrase	$0.20	Add
	Exact	$0.35	Add
you	Broad	$0.76	Add
IS: 0	Phrase	$0.26	Add
	Exact	$0.35	Add
copywriting	Broad	$0.69	Add
IS: 0	Phrase	$0.23	Add
	Exact	$0.35	Add
jill shalvis	Broad	$0.76	Add
IS: 0	Phrase	$0.26	Add
	Exact	$0.38	Add
how write novel	Broad	$0.88	Add
IS: 0	Phrase	$0.28	Add
	Exact	$0.42	Add
online business	Broad	$0.63	Add
IS: 0	Phrase	$0.23	Add
	Exact	$0.61	Add
9780205309023	Broad	$2.12	Add
IS: 0	Phrase	$0.71	Add
	Exact	$1.04	Add
writing romance	Broad	$0.89	Add
IS: 0	Phrase	$0.31	Add
	Exact	$0.44	Add
ecommerce	Broad	$1.83	Add
IS: 0	Phrase	$0.61	Add

ⓘ Some keywords are not eligible for targeting and will not show ads. Learn more

HUH?

I mean, don't get me wrong—I appreciate Amazon suggesting "books best sellers" as a key phrase and I might just try that one, but the other suggestions are pretty out there. Jill Shalvis is a romance novelist (and I'm sure she's a lovely person), but paying to advertise my book when someone types her name into Amazon is not going to get me anywhere with my non-fiction book on self-publishing. The other suggestions are just strange and generally useless— "you, online business, how, blogging, 9780205309023."

Um….ok.

Pretty sure no one typing in "you" is going to end up buying this book. I would find this kind of thing funny if I didn't know full well that authors are wasting money by trusting Amazon and adding all of these irrelevant words (with their outrageous suggested bids) into an expensive campaign that will get them no results.

That is not going to work at all, so please skip this interface as well and be happy that you saved another $1,000 by ignoring this screen. Yay!

Next, you'll need to take your list of book-related keywords from Chapter 12 and start entering them into the "Enter list" field. If you didn't do that research (and/or you don't have your seven keyword slots filled in), now is the time to stop and do that. Amazon needs that data to help your book perform better. If you didn't do that research, Publisher Rocket is a great resource.

This is also the moment where you will be introduced to one of the best-kept secrets of Amazon research— the advertising keyword auto-completion box.

FUNNY YOU SHOULD ASK: HOW TO MARKET A BOOK

Match type ⓘ ☐ Broad ☑ Phrase ☑ Exact

```
how to self publish
```

Not all of these shoppers' queries are eligible for targeting

Add keywords

how to self publish your book

how to self publish on amazon

how to self publish on amazon preliminary and pragmatic glory tsar

how to self publish a children's book

how to self publish

how to self publish your book on amazon

how to self publish a book

how to self publish your book for free and not get conned

how to self publish comics

w ads. Learn more

how to self publish a book on amazon

Add all keywords in this list

tional

CHECK THIS OUT! I put in "how to self-publish a book," and it came back with a totally useful (and relevant) list that included some phrases even I hadn't thought of! That's what I'm talking about! I can actually use these keywords to sell some books.

. . .

Don't you just love how Amazon made us jump through two sets of terrible default suggestion interfaces before showing us that, in fact, it has all of this great information? This seems unnecessarily complicated, but here we are.

This is what I do with the settings on the "enter list" tab. Switch from "suggested bid" (because again, never take their suggestions!) to "custom bid" and set the bid at something low, like 20 cents. The only way to see if you can get your ads to show for less money is to start out by offering less money, so that's why I start at 20 cents. If you can get your ads to start showing at this discounted price, you're golden!

Keyword targeting

Suggested | **Enter list** | Upload file

Bid: Custom bid $ 0.20

Match type: ☐ Broad ☑ Phrase ☑ Exact

For "match type," I will leave "phrase, and exact" checked, at least initially. If you're curious (which I'm sure you are not), a "broad" match encompasses all of the keywords you entered in any order, plus variations and related keywords; "Phrase match" CONTAINS the phrase or keywords no matter what order they are in, and "exact match" is the exact match of that keyword or key phrase. I un-check "broad," because I just don't trust Amazon to go off on its own.

Keep adding keywords from your lists and from Amazon's suggestions until you get to 100 (which is really just 50 with "phrase" and "exact" turned on). I keep the list to 100, because you're going to go back in later and see what is working—and if you have 1,000 words in each ad you're going to get overwhelmed.

Moving on! The next setting is the "Campaign Bidding strategy." Switch this to "Dynamic bids—down only," meaning you're willing to pay LESS than the bid you agreed to, but not more. The default here is "Dynamic bids— up and down," which of course you don't want because it gives Amazon the power to double your bid without asking you. Just... no.

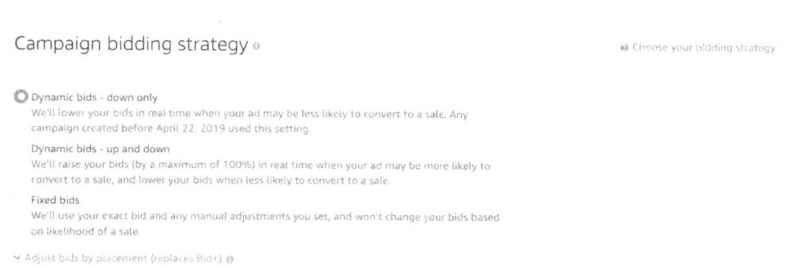

At the very bottom of the page, you'll see "Settings," which was recently moved from the top of the page for no discernible reason (other than perhaps to disorient users so they give up and leave the defaults).

Under "Campaign Name," please put the name of the book and the type of ad you are running. Eventually, you're going to be running a bunch of these ads, and if they all have very similar names, that's just going to confuse and anger you when you come back here to see what worked. Set yourself up to win by naming the ad something you can search for later.

Next is yet another of Amazon's attempts to trick you into spending a bunch of money: "no end date." YIKES. This is Amazon trying to get you to give them access to your credit card so they can charge you every day with "no end date." Does that sound like it benefits you? No, it does not.

Change "end date" to a date two or three weeks in the future. What you DON'T want is to leave "no end date" there, forget to check your ads, and end up with a surprise $1,000 ad bill at the end of the month. News flash: even if you didn't know what you were doing and just used all the defaults, you still owe that money, and no amount of claiming ignorance is going to get you out of paying the bill.

You're brand-new at this and this ad is completely unproven, so you need a controlled time window with a finite end date to keep you from getting into too much trouble. Change the date, and when Amazon sends you a friendly reminder email that your ad is about to expire, log in and see if that ad actually made you some sales before you extend the date.

Not to break my arm patting myself on the back, but that piece of advice probably just saved you another $1,000. :)

. . .

Finally, set your daily budget to $5.00, because you have to start somewhere. It's unlikely that you'll actually spend $5 per day when you first start because it's going to take a little while for Amazon to start showing your ads, but pick something you'd be OK spending!

All of that comes together to look like this:

Settings

Campaign name
How to Self Publish manual keywords 1

Portfolio
No Portfolio

Start: Jul 9, 2022
End: Jul 23, 2022

Marketplace
United States

Daily budget
$ 5.00

Save as draft   Launch campaign

Hit the "Launch campaign" button and your ad will be submitted to Amazon for review. Right away, you'll receive an email saying that your ad is in review, then after a few hours (provided your ad passes the review process, which it should), you'll receive a second email verifying that your ad is "eligible to be shown." This confuses many people, so I'll just touch on it briefly before I let you go and start your first ads.

"Eligible to be shown" is the closest Amazon can come to verifying your ad is, in fact, "live," but the "live-ness" of the ad is based on a number of factors, so the only way you'll know if the ad is actually running is to come back and check on it regularly. This has mostly to do with your bid, which I have advised you to set artificially low. The fact is, you don't know the bid threshold that is going to get your ads shown because you don't know what everyone else is bidding for their book to be shown for those terms, so it's better to start low and increase it until your ads start being shown (which you will know because your ad will start getting "impressions," and hopefully sales.

If you take the suggested bids, your ads are more likely to start running right away, but that also makes it more likely that you'll blow through your whole budget without getting any sales or useful information. By setting your bids low and increasing them incrementally until they start running, you give yourself the best chance at selling books with an advertising budget you can sustain.

Phew! That's it! You're at the end of the first type of ad I suggest you run, the "manually chosen keywords" ad. Now, if you find you're feeling particularly motivated, I'd say you should go ahead and do this process all the way through two more times— once for "Categories" to advertise your book in (which you compiled during the "Category Research" exercise in Chapter 11), and once for "Individual Products" (which is all the books from your competitive analysis and any others you might want your book to be seen for). I would love to do a detailed walk-through of each one of those ads (and just might do that in an advertising-specific book—you've been warned!), but I'm guessing you're already maxed out on ad talk and don't want this chapter to go on for another 10 pages. Let's call it here.

. . .

FUNNY YOU SHOULD ASK: HOW TO MARKET A BOOK 193

By the way, those types of ads are both located under "Manual Targeting>Product targeting," which looks like this:

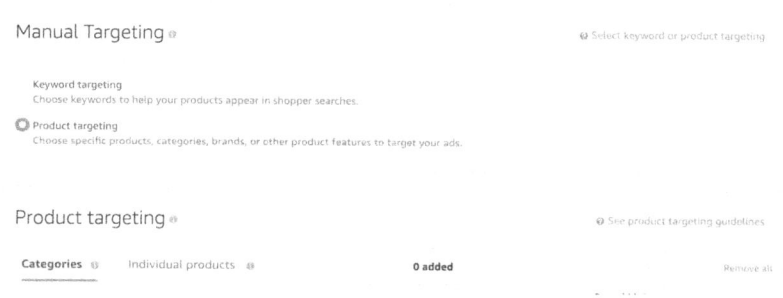

Don't get overwhelmed—just go back through this chapter and use all of the exact same settings, and most importantly, be sure to switch to "Custom Bid" instead of "Suggested." Stay away from those defaults!

That's it for Amazon Ad setup. Your next step will be to go back and check your ads on a daily basis to make sure they are running and to see if you make any sales or if you need to make changes (either to the ad campaign or the book). Ads are a "trial and error" learning process, and since you have set them up correctly, hopefully you can get up and over this learning curve quickly for as little money as possible. I have put some more information about the follow-up (like, what to do if your ads aren't showing, etc) over at https://bookpromotion.com/ads.

18

72 MORE WAYS TO PROMOTE YOUR BOOK

Y ou've waited patiently for me to tell you a bunch of ways to hustle your book out there, and here we are! I hope you can see the method to my madness here—if I had told you any of these things any sooner, you might have just jumped right in and done one (or all) of them and never come back. I didn't want that, because these promotional and marketing activities are meant to be enhancements or amplifiers of a well-optimized book by an author with a properly-constructed network. Unless and until you have these parts of your foundation in place, I don't think you should be doing random one-off promotional things, because any one of them could take off and be so successful that they get you a ton of traffic and book sales. Traffic and sales are great, but in the bigger picture, we want them to contribute to your overall career growth.

Here we go! All the promotional and marketing things.

. . .

1. Order author copies of your book. You'll need these to use for giveaways, to sell on your website, and to take with you to physical appearances.

2. Add your book to your Amazon Author Central listing. This doesn't always happen automatically!

3. Add your book's link to your LinkTree.

4. Make a 3D mockup of your book cover. Go on over to https://diybookcovers.com/3Dmockups/ and create a 3D mockup of your book cover. That will look like this:

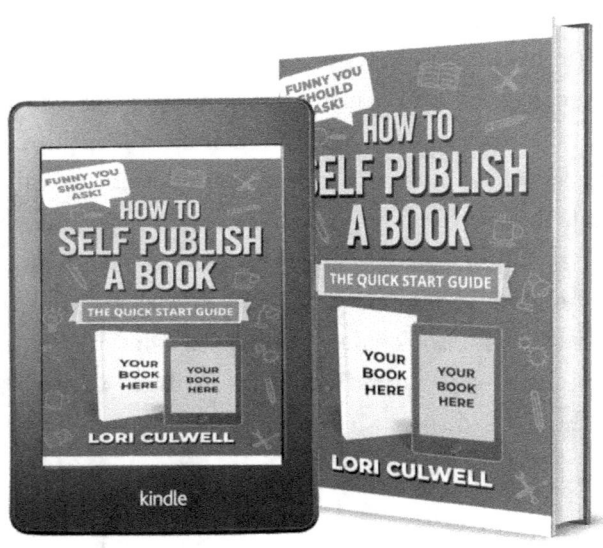

5. Post that image on your author website, with links to buy your book in all the places it is for sale. You can put your books and their links on your website in a few different ways: Use a plugin like Books Gallery or BookPress, or you can manually add all the links to the site, or you can use a tool like https://books2read.com/, which was literally created just for this exact purpose.

6. Use that image in an announcement about your book to your email list. If you have an email list, now is the absolute perfect moment to send an email to the people on that list announcing your book launch. Your list has people on it who signed up because they like you, and who also want to hear more about what you're doing, to celebrate your victories, and to cheer you on!

7. Participate in one or more email swaps so other authors will announce your book to their lists (you'll need a list to participate, obviously). Ask other authors that you know, or sign up for email swaps through paid services like BookFunnel, BookSprout, or BookSirens.

8. Put your author website in your email signature. Go over to your email provider (Gmail or whatever you use) and set it up so your author website (yourfirstnamelastname.com) will appear at the bottom of every single email you send out, right under your name.

9. Get author business cards with your website printed on them. Give them out to everyone you meet, and tell them you have a new book!

. . .

10. Make merch. If you have a beautiful character or a great catchphrase, make that into merch. Use print-on-demand sites like RedBubble or Zazzle to create everything from coffee cups to t-shirts and tote bags. Always include your author website link so new people can find you and buy your books (and get on your list!).

11. Set up a blog tour. Armed with your book cover and summary (and the fantastic press section from your author website!), start pitching yourself to genre-specific book bloggers. You can find lists of these over at https://bookpromotion.com/blog

12. Make an announcement about your book on your personal Facebook profile. You can only do this every so often, so I would recommend waiting until you have some good news about the book to share (like you've just gotten a bestseller badge or you get a great mention from a reviewer). Technically, Facebook doesn't want you using your personal profile for marketing purposes, but friends and family want to know what's going on with you!

13. Update the cover art of your Facebook business page (your author page) to include your book cover.

14. Post your book's link on your Facebook author page/business page.

15. Go live on Facebook to chat about your book.

. . .

16. Make a Facebook story about your book. You can actually do this from your profile AND your page!

17. Post about your book in Facebook groups you're active in (provided the admin says it's OK— always ask the admin first!)

18. Tweet about your book. Obviously do not do this obnoxiously or repeatedly, but if you have Twitter fans, now is the time to tell them where to get your book! You can even pin this tweet to the top of your Twitter profile so it's the first thing people see (until your next book comes out of course!).

19. If you're a fiction author, start talking about your book's genre, subgenre, and tropes on Twitter. Search by hashtags for your areas of interest, like #paranormalshifter or #yafiction. Don't say "buy my book," but do demonstrate your knowledge of that genre.

20. If you're a nonfiction author, search for people who are struggling with the things you talk about in your book and give them actual helpful solutions to their problems. When they realize what a genius you are, they will hopefully follow your links and buy your books.

21. Find your book on Amazon and pin it on Pinterest.

. . .

22. Speaking of Pinterest, make a folder named "Your Subgenre" and add your book to it (as well as other writers' books in that subgenre).

23. Make a fancy, genre-specific pin, like this:

Canva is a great graphic design resource to use for this kind of thing, with many pre-made templates in their basic free account.

24. Make a book trailer (or have one made for you).

25. Post your book trailer on your website, on all of your social media, and on your Amazon Author Central.

26. Post your book cover and link to your Instagram. Hopefully you'll already be getting shout-outs from BookStagrammers you approached as part of your ARC campaign, so be sure to update your IG the moment your book comes out.

27. Post updates about your book launch to your Instagram. Photos of your book in stores, of you at book signings, and of noteworthy things that happen in your author life (like earning a bestseller badge!) are fun for your followers to see.

28. Post book-related videos to your Instagram reels.

29. Make a "universal link" to your book using BookLinkr.

30. Go live on Instagram to chat about your book.

. . .

31. Create an Instagram story about your book (or your characters, or your writing process, or your life)

32. Encourage people to take selfies with your book and then tag you on social media.

33. Put your books in a bundle. If you have multiple books (like in a series), bundling is a great way to offer a good deal on your books and get some further exposure.

34. Write a press release about your book. Think of a good angle, like a connection to a place or a popular theme. "I wrote a book" is not necessarily a newsworthy headline, so write something that a reporter could pick up and make a story out of! You can put your press release out through PR Log (www.prlog.com).

35. Add your book link to the back matter of all your books, then republish.

36. Contact local bookstores to ask them to stock your book. This will work better if you have a decent social media following and if the paperback version of your book is also available through IngramSpark (because they allow returns).

37. Contact local bookstores to set up readings. Again, this will work better if you have a large social media following and can ensure that you will bring people into the store.

. . .

38. Set up local events. Can't or don't want to get into a bookstore? Not a problem. Contact local bars and restaurants to talk about hosting a local launch party for your book. Invite friends and local fans, and sell signed copies while you're there!

39. Post YouTube videos. If your YouTube channel is author-life focused, talk about events, accomplishments, or how your launch is going. If your channel is more focused on you as a person, start posting more videos to generate interest.

40. Make bookflips on TikTok.

41. Make other kinds of TikToks, like about the characters in your book.

42. Go live on TikTok to talk about your book.

43. Put your ebook on "permafree." Permafree is when your ebook is always free on all marketplaces. Once you're done with your initial 90-day KDP Select period, you might want to consider NOT re-enrolling, instead opting to make that book "permafree." You can find some more information on this at https://bookpromotion.com/permafree

44. Attend an in-person conference for your genre.

45. Speak at a conference for your genre.

46. Speak at an event. If you are a nonfiction author, book yourself as a speaker at one or more events related to your area of expertise. Sell physical copies of your book while you're there.

47. Start a book club on the form of social media you like the most. Talk about your own book (of course!), but also others in your genre.

48. Put your book as a publication on LinkedIn.

49. Write for Medium or other article sites.

50. Do a giveaway.

51. Add your book to "to be read" lists on GoodReads.

52. Post about your book in your GoodReads feed.

53. Put A+ content on your book's listing. In case you haven't noticed it in action, some book listings now have this kind of thing in their "From the Publisher" section, which looks like this:

From the Publisher

Or this:

As you can see, A+ is a much more visually appealing and available way of getting people to learn more about your book, and is way more elegant than the "Look Inside the Book" feature. That feature takes forever to show up after publication, plus Amazon has never been able to get that feature to work on mobile. A+ is much better because it gives you the chance to show and describe the book on the actual listing rather than requiring the customer to do more work to look inside. Fantastic!

Here's a tutorial on A+ content if you would prefer to watch a step by step video: https://bookpromotion.com/aplus

54. Pitch yourself to podcasts. If you think your book's subject matter is a fit, reach out to podcasts to make appearances. Visit https://podcastguests.com or Google "your subject + podcast."

55. Start your own podcast. Can't find the right podcast? Start one! Internet marketing guru Pat Flynn has an excellent tutorial over at https://www.smartpassiveincome.com/guide/how-to-start-a-podcast-tutorial-pat-flynn/

56. Hire a publicist. If you have done everything in this book and you have disposable income, feel free to hire a publicist! It is super fun to have your book mentioned in the media and it does increase book sales (somewhat, a little bit). It's not a cure-all, but if media exposure is an experience that you want and you can afford it, then by all means, hire a publicist! Here's a database: https://reedsy.com/publicity/book-publicist

. . .

Before you hire anyone, make sure you do your research:

—Get references, and actually contact them.

—Be sure they have worked with authors before.

—Be clear on your agreement. What will happen if they don't get you on TV or radio as promised?

—Ask for a firm timeframe.

—Ask that they give you details about whom they will approach on your behalf.

57. Approach famous authors in your genre. If they love your work, they might be willing to give you a blurb for your book, tell their network about you, and/or offer you some mentoring. It never hurts to ask!

58. Talk about your book! Get in the habit of saying "I wrote a book!" to new people that you meet. You need to get that momentum going somehow, even if it is one person at a time. The next time you end up talking to a stranger in line at the drugstore, be sure to mention that you are a published author. Give them your business card!

. . .

59. Put your next book on pre-order (even if it's not done yet). Both KDP and IngramSpark have the ability to put books on pre-order, and the reason to do this is to catch people while they're excited about your work and want to buy something else right then. Give them what they want!

60. Reach out to local media, either in your town, your hometown, or the town where your book is set. Locality is an interesting angle and reporters who cover what's referred to as local color might want to cover your book (or you) in relation to the town.

61. Get a booth at a local fair, event, farmer's market, or anywhere large groups of people go. You'll need your author copies and some signage for this kind of thing, and be sure to bring your business cards!

62. Get in touch with your local library. Many libraries will let you do readings (especially if you wrote a children's book), so reach out to them and ask!

63. Ask your library system if they will carry your book. If they say yes, donate signed copies.

64. Hire an influencer to promote your book. Find an influencer with a large audience of your target audience members and reach out to them to see if they will mention your book. Depending on the size of their following, they will let you know how much they charge for this.

. . .

65. Write guest blogs. Google "your genre + blog," and reach out to the owners of the websites you find. This will obviously be much easier if you are a nonfiction author.

66. Do a giveaway. This will help you get email sign ups to your list.

67. Run a Kindle countdown deal. If you decide to stay with KDP Select and put your book in Kindle Unlimited instead of going wide with your distribution. Be sure to either use your free days or do a Kindle countdown deal every quarter. If you are going to be exclusive to Amazon, you should get as much out of it as possible.

68. Publish your book on Kobo, then use their promotional tools to run a deal.

69. Put your book on wider distribution using draft2 digital, PublishDrive, or IngramSpark (or all three!)

70. Work on your reader magnet. If you're not getting a lot of signups from your book, improve your reader magnet!

71. Have paper postcards printed up and walk around putting them on people's cars.

. . .

72. Make a Facebook Page dedicated to the genre of your book. The explanation for this became so lengthy, it grew into its own chapter, which is next.

As you can see, there are countless ways to promote your book. I'm sure you can think of some that I haven't covered here! The bottom line is finding something that works for you and doing it consistently.

PART 4: POST-LAUNCH ACTIVITIES

 We're back at the beginning now, in the interim time between the launch and marketing of your current book and your next book. What can you do while you're in the process of writing and editing your next big project?

I'm so glad you asked me that! I have some ideas (of course!).

19
START A FACEBOOK PAGE + GROUP ABOUT YOUR GENRE/SUBGENRE

Build a Facebook Group + Page (Not About Yourself or Your Books)

This chapter (and the method I describe in it) involves Facebook and requires that you have at least a Facebook account and a little bit of familiarity with how that platform works. If you don't use Facebook because you're too young (I get it) or you feel like the target audience for your genre/subgenre isn't on Facebook, feel free to skip ahead. This method works great for some people and not at all for others.

Now that I have that disclaimer out of the way, let me issue another one: I'm going to encourage you to do a thing right now that you might find strange, but hear me out. We are about to make a group where you are going to promote other people's books.

. . .

Remember when I said way back in chapter one that I don't think social media sells books? I still stand behind that statement when it comes to author-specific social media. I do still think authors need social media profiles as part of their author platforms, and for reputation management purposes, but I'm not saying you're going to sell books that way. I have tried for years to sell books using author-specific social media profiles (mine and others). It doesn't work that well, for two reasons:

The first issue is that social media companies want your money. They exist to make money for themselves, so they're going to find every way possible to charge you if they see you blatantly trying to make money for yourself (like by selling books from an author or book page). That is why it is so very, very difficult to grow your page.

If it makes you feel any better, I have managed social media for several famous authors in my role as a publishing and marketing consultant, and even THEY have trouble growing their social media and selling books on those pages. Social media (and in this example, I specifically mean Facebook) wants you to spend money to buy ads and boost your posts. They don't care if you sell books or build up your fanbase.

The second problem is that when you first start out as an author, no one knows about you, so no one knows to search for you to find you organically for the types of books you write. Ideally, one day your name will become synonymous with "cozy mysteries" or whatever you write, but that day is not today, so it's very unlikely that a random cozy mystery lover is going to happen upon your Facebook page and then buy your books. Facebook is certainly not going to recommend your author page to cozy mystery lovers (without financial incentive), and because of the first problem I mentioned, even if you do pay to build that audience up, they're still going to charge you to talk to them. Having to pay multiple times like that to acquire a potential customer and then engage them practically guarantees that you will never achieve a positive return on investment (ROI) on your books.

Here's the problem in a nutshell: You're not going to become a famous author unless a lot of people buy your books, but where are you supposed to get a lot of people that want to buy your books so you can become a famous author?

The good news is, that I have a method that will help. But before we dive in (and I know I sound like a broken record here), do not start this until you already have your email signup with your reader magnet ready to go. It's useless to gather up a bunch of potential customers and then have no way to capture them on your email list. Remember, social media is great, but it can still go away at a moment's notice.

Here's the deal. While people aren't searching for you yet, you know what they ARE searching for? Keywords that reflect your genre/subgenre.

Here is some proof of that:

. . .

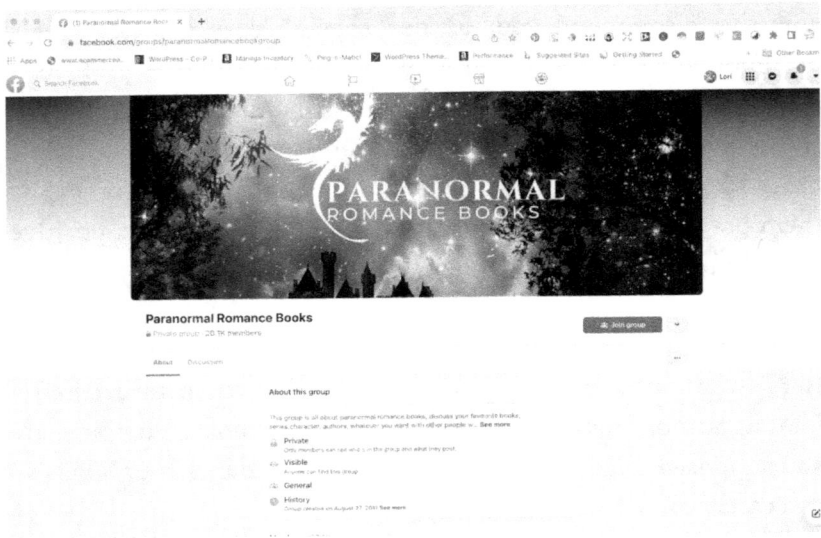

Wow! 21,000 people, all talking about paranormal romance! That's amazing! That is a ton of people who are interested in that genre and will probably want to buy that type of book. Your first thought might be to join this group and see if you can get the owner to let you post a link to your book. If you can make that happen, that actually would be a great way to promote your book.

However, I'm guessing that the person that runs this group has a "no spam or promotion" policy, so it's highly unlikely they're going to let you do that—and if you try to do it anyway, you're going to get yourself kicked out of that group.

Now, don't get me wrong, I still think you should join groups like this, because these people are your actual readers and you might be able to make friends with some of them and get them to read your ARCs, but that's going to take a ton of time and has to be done very slowly and carefully.

So here's a better approach: Start your own group.

In my opinion, this is a much better use of your time, because then you'll have the entire group (and all of its members) as your captive audience, and you can promote your stuff to them as you see fit. Plus, if the group is about something you like and are passionate about, you'll likely enjoy engaging with it. It's really a win-win.

Great! You're convinced. So then, how to set up and grow an engaged group? I'm going to tell you, but before I do, I will warn you that this example gets a little hairy and technical, so I'll do my best to make it funny whenever possible. Deep breath.

To be very clear, I am suggesting that instead of trying to grow social media accounts about yourself and your books, you instead focus on growing an engaged group of people who like your genre and/or subgenre, get them actively engaged in discussions (including talk of your competitors' books!), and then eventually use the page and group to promote your own books, since you'll know these people are fans of that genre.

The big secret of this chapter is that Facebook groups are where the real engagement happens, but the only way to grow a Facebook group is (of course) to start a Facebook Page and run paid advertising to it, then invite all of those people over to the group to talk about that topic. Yes, Facebook is going to get your money somehow, and I am in fact telling you to give money to Facebook, but the difference here is that instead of it being a one-time, one-shot gamble like a Facebook to Amazon ad for your book, this will be a Facebook ad targeted at acquiring people who are fans of your genre, which is much more cost-effective. What you're doing with this method is building an engaged community, which will be a long-term asset for your career.

Here's how that goes, using my own Facebook page and group for book marketing and promotion strategies as a real-life example. Also, let's just acknowledge right now that this is the world's most meta example, because this is a book about book marketing, and here I am trying to teach you book marketing methods by showing you a Facebook page and group dedicated to book marketing which I realize will eventually serve as book marketing for my book marketing book.

We have disappeared down the rabbit hole of book marketing, people. We're there.

I write books about self-publishing and book marketing, so it makes sense for me to have a group like this where I can lead and comment on book marketing discussions. I didn't call the page and group "Buy Lori Culwell's Books!" because a) no one is searching for that term, and b) I'm trying to build a community of authors who want to learn more about marketing and get advice about how to sell more books. I'm building on subject matter here. Do people eventually buy my books on self-publishing and book marketing after they see that I know what I'm talking about? Yes, they do and I appreciate every single sale. My point is that I built the page and the group around the subject, not myself.

. . .

1. First, start a Facebook group. https://www.facebook.com/groups/. You do that by clicking this button right here:

Mine looks like this:

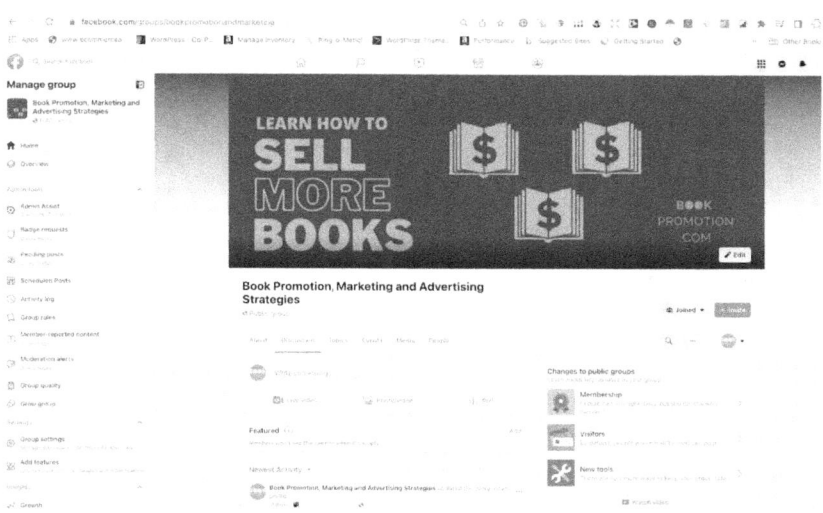

Fill out all of the information (description, website if you have one, etc), flesh out the group with some actual good content (like photos and links), upload a photo, and invite any friends you think might actually enjoy this group. (But don't spam your friends!)

Also, is now a good time to say that you should totally join my free Facebook group? It's really fun, and I love talking about book marketing. https://www.facebook.com/groups/bookpromotionandmarketing

2. Take your genre/subgenre name (the best one that you came up with for your book in the exercise in Chapter 9) and use it in your group name. This is very important.

3. Next, you'll need a way to get people into your group. There is no way (yet) to advertise a group on Facebook, so you'll create a "mirror" Facebook page using the exact same content.

To start a Facebook page, go to https://www.facebook.com/pages and look for this button:

+ Create new Page

My book marketing page looks like this:

FUNNY YOU SHOULD ASK: HOW TO MARKET A BOOK 223

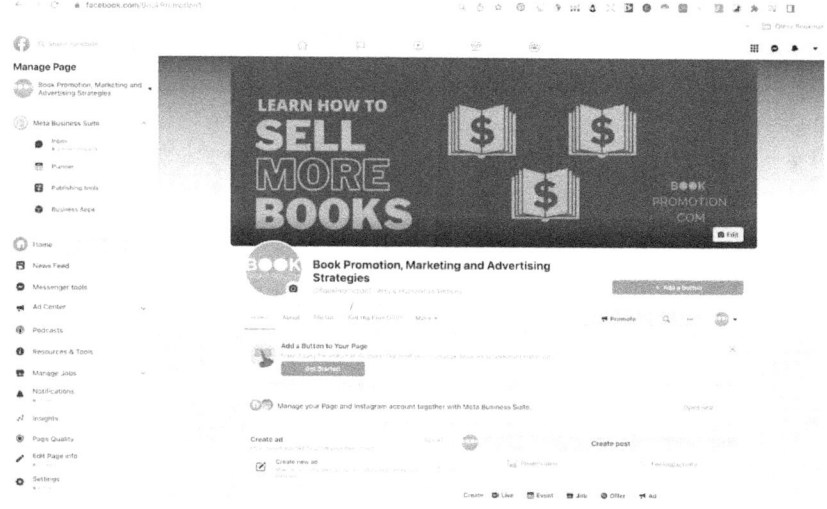

Next you need to link the page to the group, like this:

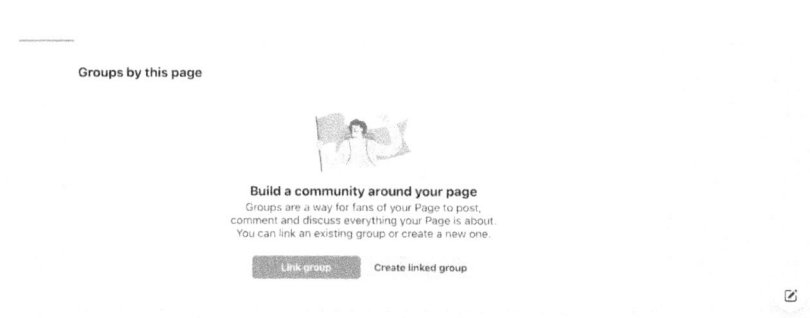

Once the page and group are linked, head back to the page and click "Create ad." You're going to be taking out a paid ad with the goal of getting people to like the page. I'm also mentioning the group in the ad, just for fun.

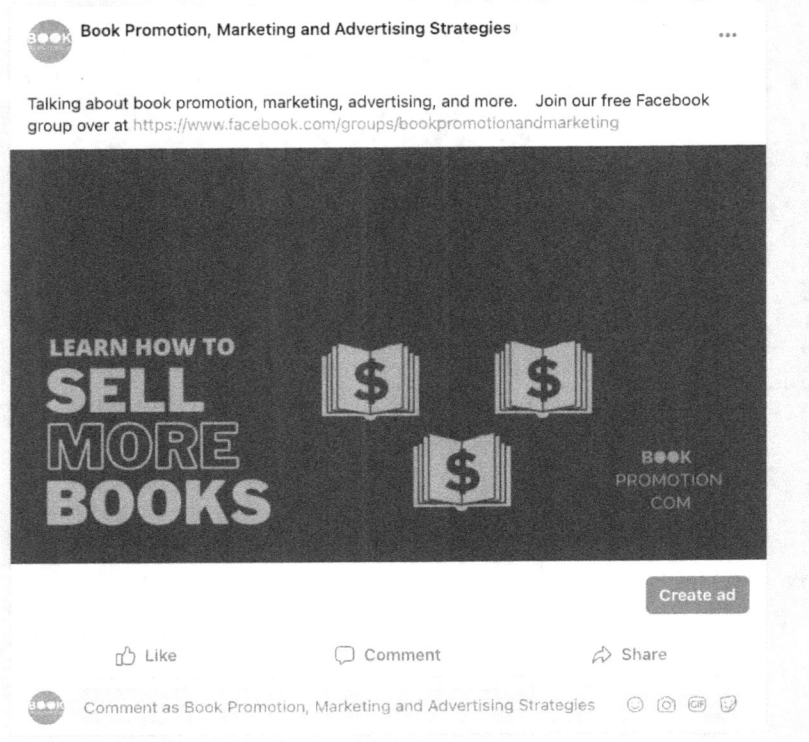

I know, this is getting super technical. Frankly I'm shocked if you've made it this far and are trying to actually do this method, so I'm going to just truncate the "Ad Settings" steps here so you can set this up as a test to see if this is even something you're going to want to do going forward.

Under "Goal," you'll switch from the default over to "Get more page likes" (engagement).

. . .

Under "Button," switch to "No Button," since you're trying to get page likes.

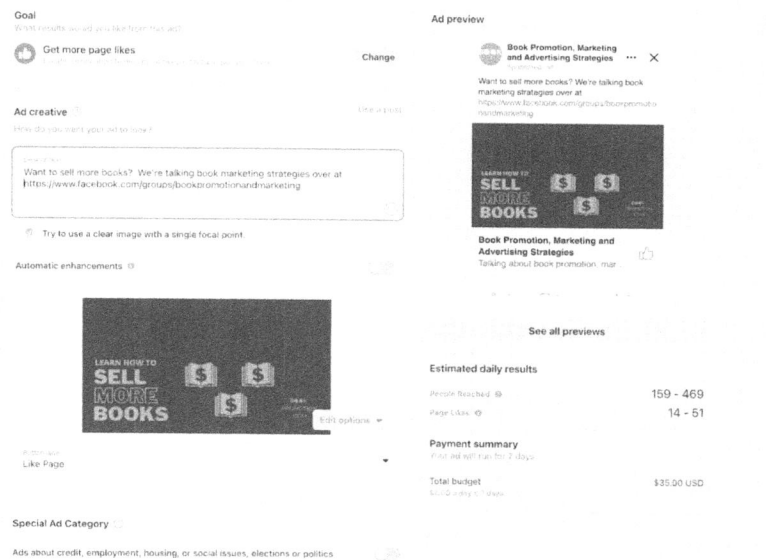

Build an "Audience" and save it. I'm targeting men and women, ages 40-65+, because I know that to be the demographic of people who have the time and money to self-publish and market a book. I'm targeting the United States because that is where the majority of my Amazon sales are going to come from, but you can expand this to any country where you'd like to build up an audience.

Edit audience

Age

40 —————————————— 65+

Selecting an audience under 18 will limit your targeting options to location, age, and gender. Learn more

Locations

Locations
Type to add more locations

United States
United States + 25 mi ×

Detailed targeting

Detailed targeting
Add people who match at least one of the following   Browse →

Interests
E-books ×   Publishing ×   Bookselling ×   Self-publishing ×
Books ×   Writing ×

Demographics
Amazon Kindle Direct Publishing ×   BookBub ×

Suggested for you
Arts, Entertainment, Sports and Media +

For advanced targeting features, go to Ads Manager.

Audience definition
Your audience selection is fairly broad.

Specific ———————————————— Broad

Estimated audience size: 88M - 103.5M

★ Potential Reach is now Estimated Audience Size

Estimated Audience Size is an estimate of the range of people who match your targeting criteria. You can use this estimate to better understand how your targeting selections can limit or expand your audience size. This estimate may vary over time based on available data. You may see improved performance with a broader audience definition. Learn more

Cancel   **Save audience**

Finally, you'll designate the placement as "Facebook," since you're just building a Facebook page and not advertising a product. Your only goal here is to get people to like the page so you can show them your products (and pull them over to the group).

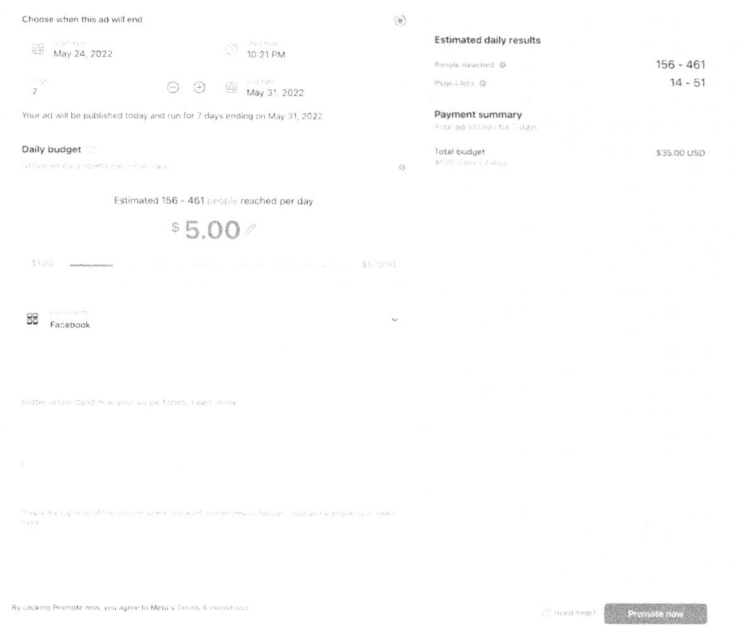

Hit the blue "Promote now" button, then you're done with the ad. Facebook will email you when it has been approved and is running. You're only paying for actual likes on the page.

Once your ad goes live, you'll be notified when you get new likes on the page. When you get to 1,000 people that "like" the page, you can go over to the linked group and invite those new people to become group members.

Here's how you do that:

Since both the page and the group belong to you, you're free to promote your books on them anytime you want. Just be sure to intersperse promotional links with actual interesting content that encourages engagement so members don't feel like you're just there to sell them something. Groups of like-minded people love to have discussions about that subject matter, so be sure to engage them with daily questions and topic-related discussions. If you want to save yourself time, schedule your posts a week or so in advance by clicking the little calendar icon at the bottom-right corner of your post.

. . .

Now, you may be wondering why we're doing all this instead of just making a page and leaving it at that. I have found that just making a subject matter-specific Facebook Page is not all that effective anymore, because Facebook will charge you to build the page, then charge you again to engage the people you've just paid to acquire. Groups have a much higher rate of engagement because they are meant to be discussion-based, so you're basically gathering a large group of people with similar interests in the same place and introducing topics to get them coming back to have discussions. You're essentially training the Facebook algorithm to show your posts to that audience, which hopefully means that when you eventually ask them to buy your book, they will.

Does this seem like a bunch of work without a guaranteed payoff? Yes. But it is an effective strategy if you have the time and money to do it right, and I wanted to cover it here (and I thought just saying "start a Facebook page" would be aggravatingly vague advice for you).

So, that's it! Create an interest-specific Facebook page, run paid ads to grow that audience, invite those people to your Facebook group, and engage them regularly. Eventually, you'll have a group of people who like that thing and you can sell them stuff.

20
BOOK MARKETING: DAILY TASKS

Look, I know this whole book has been a heavy lift, with a ton of moments that feel like we're just seeing the proverbial tip of the iceberg, and I apologize for that. But the good news is, once you have everything set up properly (meaning your email list, landing page, and author website), book marketing is actually pretty simple and can be done as part of your daily routine. Even better, every book launch going forward should be easier than the last.

Here are some daily marketing activities you can do in between launches! If you're procrastinating on writing or editing anyway (you say, *Wait! How did you know?*), instead of reorganizing the sock drawer, do one of these things instead:

1. Try to get more people onto your list. If you're a non-fiction author, up your participation on social media (groups, pages, subreddits, TikTok) for your topic. If you write fiction, become

more active on social media, start a Facebook page (or join one) for your genre and participate in that, or join a book club to make friends with people who read that type of book. If you're not writing, be thinking about expanding your audience!

2. Write an interesting blog post or post something on your social media.

3. Start some paid ads. If your book is properly optimized and your platform is set up for growth, there is no reason to wait on setting up paid ads. If you have a chunk of downtime, get in there and spend an afternoon working through the setup process. Remember, every sale is an opportunity to get people onto your list and make them your superfans!

4. Check your ads. If you're already running paid advertising on your books, you'll need to log in frequently to see how it's doing, cut any campaigns or words that aren't working, and so on. The more you refine your ads, the better they will work and the more profit you'll make per book. Keep working on ads until you get them dialed in!

5. Email your list. If you haven't quite mastered the once-a-week communication strategy yet, practice pre-writing some broadcast messages when you have free time. Email marketing (and all marketing, really) gets easier the more you practice it, and the best time to practice is when the stakes are low and you don't need anything.

. . .

6. Learn a new skill. Have you always wanted to learn more about graphic design, social media, paid advertising, or email marketing? If you're in between books, take a course on one of these things. Now that your network is set up properly, anything you do will have a compounding effect on your entire network.

7. Review some books on Pubby. If you're going to go with Pubby to get reviews on your books, you need to spend some time building up what are called "snaps" by reviewing books. There's a cap on how many reviews you can do per week (probably to limit review posting velocity on Amazon), so if you need a bunch of reviews, it's good to keep your account active and build up your snaps in between launches.

8. Pre-schedule your content. If you have a chunk of time, take a couple of hours and schedule a month's worth of blog posts, social media posts, etc.

9. Clean up your social media act. When you have downtime, go through and delete anything that is outdated or embarrassing. This includes (but is certainly not limited to) links that are now broken, observations that you thought were witty at the time, and questionable old photos of you. You'll thank me when your book goes viral and you're not stuck triaging this while wondering if you said anything in the past ten years that could get you canceled. Another thing you can do on your social media is unfollow people who have not followed you back or have never interacted with you. Clean it up!

. . .

10. Repost good stuff. Once someone says something nice about your book or you get a bestseller badge, distribute that as far and wide as possible. Take a screenshot and post it on your Amazon Author Central. Tell your list about it. Make a blog post dedicated to it. Post it on all of your social. That way you're not just celebrating your success, you're also keeping your entire author platform active, which is important to the algorithm gods at both Google and Amazon.

11. Search for fans on social media. Repeat the exercise in Chapter 14 (ARC Team) where you search for authors who write what you write and follow their followers.

12. Start writing your next book. Since your network is now set up properly and you're always getting new people onto your list, definitely work on that next book, which is going to have a built-in audience when it launches, thanks to all the work you're doing here!

21
CONCLUSION: YOUR BIG MOMENT

You made it! Congratulations. You now know everything I know about book marketing. I hope you had at least a couple of good "aha!" moments that pertained to your book marketing life. I hope you're feeling empowered and amazing, and that you have already started selling more books!

This is the part where I would ordinarily sign off with some grand conclusion and tell you how proud I am of you (which I totally am!), but this isn't really the end. I want to hear from you! Do you have questions? How is your book marketing going? Perhaps most importantly, tell me about your successes (no matter how small)! Book marketing is an ongoing and quickly-evolving discipline, so I would love for you to come over to https://bookpromotion.com to see what I have going on over there. I do some amusing experiments on my own books over there, then write about them. All for your benefit and amusement.

. . .

And, of course, if this guide has just changed your life and you would simply like to say a nice thing or leave a review (which you can do by clicking right here or by visiting https://bookpromotion.com/book), that would also be amazing! I can't wait to hear from you!

22
WHAT ELSE CAN I TEACH YOU?

If you have enjoyed our time together so much that you would like to read some other stuff I've written, here are some other books in the "Funny You Should Ask" series!

How to Make a Website: the 100% Not-Boring Guide to Setting Up Your Website with Wordpress

How to Do Search Engine Optimization: SEO for Marketing, Blogging, and More

How to Self-Publish a Book: Getting Your Book Out There on Amazon and Beyond

How to Publish Low Content Books: Publishing Journals, Notebooks, and More on KDP

· · ·

How to Sell More Books: The Missing Piece of Your Author Marketing Strategy

www.ingramcontent.com/pod-product-compliance
Lightning Source LLC
LaVergne TN
LVHW010315070526
838199LV00065B/5566